THE
LOTUS® 1-2-3®
BOOK

D1519169

ELECTRONIC LEARNING FACILITATORS, INC.

HBJ

HARCOURT BRACE JOVANOVICH, PUBLISHERS

San Diego   New York   Chicago   Austin   Washington, D.C.
London   Sydney   Tokyo   Toronto

ISBN: 0-15-551190-4

Library of Congress Catalog Card Number: 88-83503

Printed in the United States of America

Introduction

This manual introduces you to Lotus 1-2-3, a powerful tool for managing numeric data. The "1-2-3" stands for the three major components of this software package: spreadsheet creation and manipulation, data management, and graphics. Through hands-on activities, you will learn how to create, format, save, retrieve, print, and graph spreadsheets; create, store, and manipulate a Lotus database; create a macro library; and use calendar, logical, statistical, and financial functions.

By covering all the material in this manual you will gain mastery of the basic Lotus 1-2-3 features. Specifically, you will be knowledgeable in the following areas:

- SPREADSHEETS:

    Load Lotus 1-2-3 and access the Lotus menu

    Create, save, and retrieve a spreadsheet

    Quit 1-2-3 and exit Lotus

    Enter labels, values, formulas, and functions

    Edit data

    Format a spreadsheet

    Insert new rows and columns

    Set and alter column width

    Define and manipulate cell ranges

    Use the Lotus Help facility

    Copy labels, values, and formulas

    Set up input cells for what-if analysis

    Use absolute and relative references

    Generate new data

- PRINTING AND GRAPHICS:

    Print a spreadsheet

    Generate graphs from spreadsheet data

    Print graphs using PrintGraph

- SUMMARY SPREADSHEETS:

  Understand templates

  Name ranges and combine files

- DATABASE MANAGEMENT:

  Create, sort, and query a database

  Use DATE arithmetic

  Extract data

- MACROS:

  Create, document, execute, and debug macros

  Make a macro library

  Design and create macro menus

  Use macro keywords to control program flow

  Create an automatically loading macro and an automatically executing macro

- ADVANCED RANGE COMMANDS:

  Create a table of named ranges

  Transpose ranges

  Convert ranges to values

- FUNCTIONS:

  Use calendar functions and date arithmetic

  Select from two alternatives with the @IF function

  Select from a list with the @CHOOSE function

  Construct a lookup table with the @VLOOKUP function

  Explore mathematical, statistical, and financial functions

  Use database statistical functions

  Create data tables with one and two variables

Guide to the Use of the Manual

The following conventions have been used in this manual:

- Keys to be pressed are specified in square brackets [], for example, the Home key is written [Home] and the Return key (Enter key) is written [R].

- Press [Return] ONLY when you see [R]. Some entries are shown on several lines for clarity; make the complete entry before pressing [Return].

- All capitals denote:

  Commands, for example, FILE RETRIEVE or /FR.
  Names of files and ranges, for example, EXPENSE, DATA.
  Functions, for example, @SUM.
  Cell addresses, for example, A1..B12.

- All *Activities* are presented in a two-column format:

  The left column describes the *Task* to be done.
  The right column details the *Procedure* (actual keys to press).

  In most activities the procedure column is divided into two additional columns.

  Cell location (if specified) indicates where the cell pointer is to be placed before pressing any key.
  Enter indicates exactly what you are to enter.

- " " surround text to be entered. Enter only the text inside, not including the quotation marks.

- < > surround data you should furnish, for example, <your name>. Do not type the brackets.

- { } indicate macros.

- Illustrations of completed spreadsheets may differ from yours. Calculated numbers may differ slightly, depending on whether or not your version is set to round off. In exercises using dates compared with the present date in the computer, your answer will differ from the illustration.

- Never enter spaces in Lotus commands. Press the Enter or Return key only when you see [R] in the instructions. Instructions for entering keystrokes may be on more than one line, or may contain spaces to make them easier to read. DO NOT ENTER SPACES.

The Student Disk

Your instructor has been provided with a student disk which he or she can copy for your use. The student disk contains the following files for use in the Activities:

EXPENSE
EXPENSES
DEPT1
DEPT2
DEPT3
SUMMARY
EMPLOYEE
SALES
DSTATS
TABLE

The disk also has these additional files for use in Case Study 3 in Unit VII on Database Management:

ABLE
BAKER
CHARLIE
BOXFACT

Students are instructed to save their work under other names such as EXPENSE1 and SUMMARY2. Please ensure that you make a backup copy of the student disk before using the files, to avoid overwriting them.

CONTENTS

x

xii

UNIT·1·

Introduction to Electronic Spreadsheets

Overview: This module introduces you to the basic features of spreadsheets and the advantages of electronic spreadsheets over paper and pencil ones. It also introduces the Lotus Access System and the 1-2-3 program.

Skills: Spreadsheets as tables of related data

Loading Lotus 1-2-3

Moving the cell pointer

Creating a simple spreadsheet

Saving a spreadsheet

Quitting 1-2-3 and exiting Lotus

Retrieving a spreadsheet

Changing cell values

Model: The model used in this introductory module is a simple personnel spreadsheet.

Spreadsheet Basics

A spreadsheet is a table of columns and rows. In Lotus 1-2-3 columns have letters and rows have numbers. The intersection of a column and a row is called a *cell*. Each cell has a unique cell address. The cell at the intersection of column E, row 9 has the cell address E9. In the spreadsheet below, cell E9 contains a number, 24500.

Entire rows or columns or any rectangular group of cells is called a *range* and is identified by the top and bottom cell (column), the left and right cell (row), or the upper left cell and the lower right cell. Cell ranges in the spreadsheet below would be:

Column A: A1..A9

Row 7:   A7..E7

Whole spreadsheet: A1..E9

	A	B	C	D	E
1	Name:		<your name>		
2	Date:		<today's date>		
3	Subject:		Employee Ages and Salaries		
4					
5	Name		Age		Salary
6					
7	Adams, John		38		35000
8	Smith, Susan		45		42000
9	Jones, Randy		23		24500

Spreadsheet entries fall into one of the following categories:

- Numbers (values)
- Text (labels)
- Formulas (relationships between/among cells)
- Functions

Accessing Lotus 1-2-3

The Lotus 1-2-3 human interface presents the user with a series of menus. The menus allow you to select choices in one of two ways: by pressing the first letter of a choice (giving a command), or by highlighting the choice by using the arrow keys located on the numeric keypad and pressing the [Return] key [R] to confirm (pointing to a choice).

The Lotus Access Menu is the gateway to all Lotus activities. From this menu you can select from the following:

1-2-3	Selects the Lotus 1-2-3 spreadsheet.
PrintGraph	Allows you to print graphs you have saved on your disk.
Translate	Allows you to translate from Lotus 1-2-3 Release 2 to other program formats.
Install	Allows you to configure Lotus for particular types of computers and peripherals (monitors, printers, etc.).
View	Allows you to use an on-disk introduction and overview of Lotus 1-2-3.
Exit	Allows you to leave Lotus and return to DOS.

Activity 1-1: Loading Lotus 1-2-3

In the activity that follows, you will load Lotus 1-2-3 from the Lotus Access System.

	Procedure	
Task	**Cell Location**	**Enter**
Turn on your computer and monitor. Load DOS if it is not on your Lotus system disk.		
Load the Lotus program.		LOTUS [R]
Use the arrow keys to explore the Access Menu—Do not make a selection yet.		

	Procedure	
Task	**Cell Location**	**Enter**
Select 1-2-3		1 or highlight 1-2-3 and [R]

A blank spreadsheet appears on the screen. Note that the rows are numbered and the columns labeled with letters.

Moving Around the Spreadsheet

The upper left cell is highlighted when the spreadsheet is loaded. The highlighting is done by the *cell pointer*. The cell pointer can be moved to any cell, thus highlighting it. Cell pointer moves are controlled both by pressing single keys and by key combinations.

Key	Action
[right arrow]	Moves cell pointer one cell to right.
[left arrow]	Moves cell pointer one cell to left.
[up arrow]	Moves cell pointer up one cell.
[down arrow]	Moves cell pointer down one cell.
[PgDn]	Moves cell pointer down one page (20 rows).
[PgUp]	Moves cell pointer up one page.
[Ctrl][right arrow]	Moves cell pointer one page to right.
[Ctrl][left arrow]	Moves cell pointer one page to left.
[Home]	Move cell pointer to upper left corner.
[F5]	Goes directly to the specified cell address.

Activity 1-2: Creating a Simple Spreadsheet

Data is entered in a spreadsheet by:

1. Moving the cell pointer by using the arrow keys to the cell into which data is to be entered (cell location).

2. Typing the entry.

3. Pressing the [Enter] (or [Return]) key [R], or moving the cursor to another cell.

If you make a mistake, simply repeat the data entry process. Typing over data is the easiest way of changing it.

Enter the data shown below. Move around the sheet by using the cell pointer movement keys (arrow keys). As you move from cell to cell, note how the address of the cell under the pointer appears in the upper left corner of the screen.

	A	B	C	D	E
1	Name:		Margaret Brown		
2	Date:		<today's date>		
3	Subject:		Employee Ages and Salaries		
4					
5	Name		Age		Salary
6					
7	Adams	John	38		35000
8	Smith	Susan	45		42000
9	Jones	Randy	23		24500

Accessing the Menu and Saving the Worksheet

Lotus 1-2-3 is menu-driven. All the commands needed to make Lotus work are available in menus. Upon loading Lotus, an Access Menu appears on the screen, allowing you to select the part of Lotus desired. When you select 1-2-3, a blank spreadsheet appears on the screen, and the menu disappears.

In order to access the menu, press the Slash key [/]. Selecting items from the menu is as simple as pressing the first letter of the command (such as in S for Save), or moving the cursor to highlight your selection, then pressing the Return [R] or Enter key, to complete the process.

Several levels of menu may be accessed. To back out of the menu, press the Escape key [Esc] as many times as needed.

It is very important to continually save new data entered on your worksheet. When data is first entered, it remains in RAM (Random Access Memory) and is lost when power to the computer is turned off or interrupted, unless you save it to disk. You may also lose data you have entered into a spreadsheet and neglected to save by loading another file, or by exiting Lotus. To save data to disk, access the menu [/], select File [F], then Save [S], and type a filename under which your worksheet will be saved. Make it a habit to save frequently. The command is usually written /FS.

Retrieving a file that has been saved to disk is done the same way. Press the slash to get the menu, select File, then Retrieve. When prompted for a filename, select one from the menu by highlighting it and pressing [R], or by typing in the name. The command is written /FR.

The default drive and directory will be provided on the screen when you are prompted to enter the name of the file you wish to save or retrieve. If you wish to save or retrieve a file on a different drive or directory, press [Esc] as many times as necessary to clear the drive and directory information, then type the filename with the new drive or directory preceding it, for example, a:filename or c:\newdirectory\ filename.

Activity 1-3: Saving Data, Quitting 1-2-3, and Exiting Lotus

| | Procedure | |
Task	Cell Location	Enter
Save the worksheet under the name Salaries.		/FS SALARIES [R]
Quit 1-2-3.		/QY
Exit Lotus.		EY

Note: Never enter spaces in Lotus commands. Press the Enter or Return key only when you see [R] in the instructions. Instructions for entering keystrokes may be on more than one line, or may contain spaces to make them easier to read. DO NOT ENTER SPACES.

On Your Own: Loading and Exiting Lotus 1-2-3

Task

1. Load Lotus 1-2-3.

2. Retrieve the file you have just saved.

3. Change Jones to Brown.

4. Save the file under the same filename replacing the previous version.

5. Quit 1-2-3.

6. Exit Lotus.

Summary: Introduction to Electronic Spreadsheets

- A spreadsheet is an array (table) of columns and rows.

- The intersections of columns and rows are called cells.

- Columns are labeled with letters and rows with numbers allowing easy reference to cells.

- Rectangular pieces of a spreadsheet are called ranges.

- The Lotus Access System provides a menu for using the various Lotus components.

- The Lotus human interface allows choices to be made in a command or pointing fashion.

- The spreadsheet cell pointer highlights the active cell or range and is controlled with the numeric keypad.

Quick Check: Introduction to Electronic Spreadsheets

1. How do you move the cell pointer to the A1 cell with one keystroke?

2. What cell is directly below the cell D6?

3. How many cells are in the range A2..D5?

4. How do you retrieve a file from disk?

5. How do you save a file to disk?

UNIT·2·

Building a Spreadsheet

Overview: In this unit you will build a simple budget spreadsheet while incorporating most of the basic spreadsheet skills.

Skills: Planning a worksheet

Spreadsheet values, labels, and formulas

Entering and editing data

Entering formulas and functions

Defining cell ranges

Exploring the HELP facility

Using the Lotus command menu

Completed Model

		A	B	C	D	E	F	G
1	Name:		Jane Doe					
2	Date:		\<today's date\>					
3	Subject:		Budget Projections					
4								
5								
6			Current					
7			Average		Projected Quarterly Expenses			
8			Quarterly					
9	Item		Expenses	1	2	3	4	Total
10								
11	Salaries		85000					
12	Benefits		11900					
13	Equipment		22500					
14	Service		2250					
15	Supplies		6500					
16	Rent		15000					
17	Utilities		5500					
18	Travel		4250					
19								
20	Total		152900					

Planning and Documenting Your Lotus Spreadsheet

Before entering any information on a 1-2-3 spreadsheet, it is advisable to draft a copy on paper of what you would like to accomplish. For example, if you want to design a spreadsheet that will show the quarterly budget of a company, you should write down first the following information on paper:

ITEM	AVERAGE QUARTERLY EXPENSES	QUARTER			
		1	2	3	4
SALARIES	85000				
BENEFITS	11900				
EQUIPMENT	22500				
SERVICE	2250				
SUPPLIES	6500				
RENT	15000				
UTILITIES	5500				
TRAVEL	4250				
TOTAL	152900				

An important aspect of spreadsheet planning is the inclusion of an area for documentation. For example, you may want to include the following information:

NAME:
DATE:
SUBJECT:

By planning your spreadsheet before turning to the computer, you will save time and aggravation later.

Entering and Editing Data

Data is entered into a Lotus 1-2-3 spreadsheet by positioning the cursor in the desired cell, typing the data, and pressing [Return] or one of the arrow keys.

1-2-3 interprets the type of entry by the first character you type. There are two different types of cell entries:

■ VALUES, consisting of

numbers,

formulas, and

functions

- LABELS, consisting of

  letters, and

  numbers which are not calculated

If you enter a:

  0 1 2 3 4 5 6 7 8 9 . + - (@ # $

1-2-3 will interpret your cell entry as a number or a formula.

If you enter an "at symbol," (@), Lotus looks for a function. All these are treated by 1-2-3 as a *value* and will be calculated.

If you type anything else, 1-2-3 treats your cell entry as textual material, a *label*, and it will not be calculated.

Combining value and label data in the same cell causes 1-2-3 to beep and go into Edit mode. Change the cell contents to conform to all value or all label data.

On the following pages, we will look in more detail at the possible types of cell entries.

Numeric Entries

Numeric entries must obey the following rules:

- Begin with:

  0 - 9

  decimal point

  dollar sign

  + or - sign

- May end with a % sign.

- May be entered in scientific notation.

Numeric entries cannot:

- Contain commas.

- Have more than one decimal point.

- Contain spaces between values.

All numeric entries are right-justified. Numeric entries can be formatted to contain commas, dollar signs, and percent signs through the Format command. The form in which the original entry was made will be retained by the program, only the screen display will differ.

Labels

A label is any text (character) or a number used as text, for example, an address. Labels are used for headings and other identifying information within a spreadsheet. They can be up to 240 characters long and will extend across the cells to the right for display as long as the neighboring cells do not contain an entry.

Unless otherwise indicated, all labels will be left justified. You will notice that Lotus adds a prefix (') to indicate you have entered a label. If you wish to enter a numeric label, you must precede the entry with the label prefix, otherwise Lotus will read the entry as a number. Other prefixes will format a label entry in a different way.

These label prefixes are:

Character	Action
'	Left justified
^	Centered
"	Right justified
\	Repeating (----------)

Note: If a neighboring cell contains spaces entered with the spacebar, text will not display. Although you see nothing in the cell, it is filled with spaces, which 1-2-3 interprets as a label. The clue is that a single quote appears in the top left of the screen when the cursor is placed on that cell. It is the label prefix automatically assigned by 1-2-3 when the space was typed as the first entry in the cell. The cell contents (spaces) must be erased with the /Range Erase (/RE) command.

Editing Data Entries

You are able to correct cell entries both before and after the information has been entered with the [Return] key.

The most basic way of correcting cell entries is to start over and retype the cell's contents.

Before pressing [Return], the entire contents of the cell can be erased by:

- Pressing the [Esc] key. This returns 1-2-3 to the Ready mode.

- Pressing the [Ctrl] and [Break] keys. This also returns 1-2-3 to the Ready mode.

- Pressing the [Backspace] key. This will erase the last character typed. By holding down this key you can erase all characters that have been typed in the cell.

After pressing [Return], the contents of a cell can be erased by:

- Retyping the new cell entry over the existing cell entry. Move the pointer to the cell to be erased and retype the new information.

- Entering the EDIT mode [F2].

Edit Mode

The Edit mode may be used before or after [Return] has been pressed to change the contents of a cell.

1-2-3 will go into the edit mode when you attempt to enter an unrecognizable formula, or numeric item.

To edit a cell entry, position the cursor at the desired cell location and press the [F2] function key.

Several events will happen:

- A second copy of the cell entry appears in the upper left corner. This is called the "edit line."

- The cursor is at the end of the cell's contents.

■ 1-2-3 will insert characters in the Edit mode. To delete, you must press the [Del] key to remove the character you are pointing to, or press [Backspace] which will delete the character to the left of the cursor.

■ Some of the keys on the keyboard take on different meaning in the Edit mode.

<u>Key</u>	<u>Action</u>
->	Moves cursor one position to the right.
<-	Moves cursor one position to the left.
[Tab]	Moves cursor five spaces right.
[Shift] [Tab]	Moves cursor five spaces left.
[Home] [End]	Moves the cursor to the beginning or end of the cell's contents.
[F9]	Converts a formula to the numeric representation of its current value. This command is irreversible.
[Esc]	Clears the Edit line and takes you out of the Edit mode.

Activity 2-1: Building a Lotus Spreadsheet

	Procedure	
<u>Task</u>	**<u>Cell Location</u>**	**<u>Enter</u>**
You may enter the Lotus spreadsheet directly from the prompt by typing 123.		123 [R]
Load the spreadsheet EXPENSE. *Note:* DO NOT ENTER SPACES in commands.		/FR EXPENSE [R]
Fill in the documentation section, B1 . . . B3.		

		Procedure	
Task		**Cell Location**	**Enter**

Enter the title, "Projected Quarterly Expenses" into D7.

Enter the column headings 1, 2, 3, and 4 with the centering character, ^. For example, ^1.

All other labels can be typed in as shown below:

	A	B	C	D	E	F	G
1	Name:	Jane Doe					
2	Date:	<today's date>					
3	Subject:	Budget Projections					
4							
5							
6		Current					
7		Average		Projected Quarterly Expenses			
8		Quarterly					
9	Item	Expenses	1	2	3	4	Total
10							
11	Salaries						
12	Benefits						
13	Equipment						
14	Service						
15	Supplies						
16	Rent						
17	Utilities						
18	Travel						
19							
20	Total						

Save your spreadsheet as EXPENSE1.   /FS EXPENSE1 [R]

Make any necessary editing changes.

Enter the values into Column B, as shown on the following page.

	A	B	C	D	E	F	G
1	Name:	Jane Doe					
2	Date:	<today's date>					
3	Subject:	Budget Projections					
4							
5							
6		Current					
7		Average		Projected Quarterly Expenses			
8		Quarterly					
9	Item	Expenses	1	2	3	4	Total
10							
11	Salaries	85000					
12	Benefits						
13	Equipment	22500					
14	Service						
15	Supplies	6500					
16	Rent	15000					
17	Utilities	5500					
18	Travel	4250					
19							
20	Total						

	Procedure	
Task	**Cell Location**	**Enter**

Make any necessary editing changes.

Save EXPENSE1.   /FS [R]

Replace the previous version.   R

Formulas

Being able to enter formulas into cells is what gives Lotus 1-2-3 its power and makes it indispensable for calculating and projecting. A formula simply contains the addresses of the cells and the mathematical operation that you want to perform. For example, to add a row of numbers such as amounts in cells A2, B2, C2, and D2 and place the result in E2, you would position the cursor at cell location E2 and type:

+A2+B2+C2+D2

Because the formula begins with a plus sign, 1-2-3 changes to Value mode.

There are five syntax rules for entering formulas:

- Formulas must begin with one of the following:

  0 - 9 . + - (@ # $

- Formulas cannot contain any blank spaces between characters.

- Formulas cannot contain commas within numbers.

- A formula cannot reference its own location. For example, the formula in A1 could not be:

  +A1+B1

  This would be a circular reference and create an error.

- Because formulas contain cell addresses, the *value* produced by the formula changes when the values in the cell addresses change.

Entering Formulas

You can enter cell references in formulas in two ways:

- Type the cell address.
- Point to the cell with the cell pointer.

To enter a formula by typing, position the cursor at the desired cell location and then begin typing.

To enter the formula that sums a range of cells by pointing:

- Position the cursor in the cell which is to contain the result.
- Type a plus sign.
- Move the cursor to the first cell to be included in the formula.
- Type another plus sign which moves the cursor back to the original cell.
- When all cell locations have been entered, press [Return].

Operators

Operators indicate arithmetic operations within a formula. The following are the operators listed in the order of precedence.

Operator	Meaning
^	Exponentiation
+, -	Positive, Negative
*, /	Multiplication, Division
+, -	Addition, Subtraction

Parentheses override precedence. Can you explain the following examples using the above table?

Formula	Result
6+4/2	8
(6+4)/2	5

Cell Ranges

When entering formulas and functions, you will often want to refer to a row, column, or block of data on which you want the formula or function to act. Any rectangular block of cells is called a *cell range* and can consist of one or many cells.

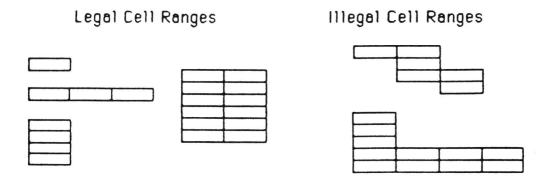

Cell ranges are described by listing the upper right and lower left cell separated by periods which defines the range as in the following examples.

Range	Definition
Single cell	A1..A1
Row of cells	A1..F1
Column of cells	A1..A25
Block of cells	A1..F25

Cell ranges are entered by either:

1. Typing the address of the defining (limiting) cells.

2. Pointing to the defining (limiting) cells.

In the Advanced Range Commands Unit, you will learn how to name cell ranges so that you can manipulate them with greater facility.

See "Cell Ranges and Range Commands" in the Appendix (page 196) for a summary of the ways in which cell ranges are used.

Activity 2-2: Entering Formulas

In the following exercise, using your EXPENSE1 file, you will create two formulas, one that will make Benefits dependent on Salary and a second that will make Service dependent on Equipment.

Task	Procedure Cell Location	Enter
Enter a formula for Benefits making it 14% of Salary.	B12	0.14*B11 [R]
Enter a formula for Service making it 10% of Equipment.	B14	0.1*B13 [R]

	Procedure	
Task	**Cell Location**	**Enter**
Sum the contents of B11..B18.	B20	+B11+B12+B13 +B14+B15+B16 +B17+B18 [R]
Save (Replace) EXPENSE1.		/FS [R] R

Your spreadsheet should look like the following:

	A	B	C	D	E	F	G
1	Name:	Jane Doe					
2	Date:	<today's date>					
3	Subject:	Budget Projections					
4							
5							
6		Current					
7		Average		Projected Quarterly Expenses			
8		Quarterly					
9	Item	Expenses	1	2	3	4	Total
10							
11	Salaries	85000					
12	Benefits	11900					
13	Equipment	22500					
14	Service	2250					
15	Supplies	6500					
16	Rent	15000					
17	Utilities	5500					
18	Travel	4250					
19							
20	Total	152900					

Functions

To make formula construction easier, 1-2-3 has a number of built-in functions. Functions are used in worksheets the same way as formulas. All functions must start with the @ symbol.

Following the @ symbol is the function's name which describes the operation to be performed. Enclosed in parentheses are the function's arguments, if required. Arguments, in the form of cell locations, range names, and other functions, tell the function on which cells to act. For example:

@SUM(B2..B4)

sums the value of items in B2, B3, and B4. Nonnumeric and blank cells are ignored.

The equivalent of +A2+B2+C2+D2 is:

@SUM(A2..D2)

Activity 2-3: Using the @SUM Function

	Procedure	
Task	Cell Location	Enter
Change the formula in B20 to the @SUM function.	B20	@SUM(B11..B18)[R]
Save (Replace) EXPENSE1.		/FS[R]R

Summary: Building a Spreadsheet

■ There are two different types of cell entries that 1-2-3 recognizes: VALUES (numbers, formulas, and functions) and LABELS (text).

■ You may edit cell entries by retyping the cell contents or by using the [F2] key.

■ 1-2-3 allows you to enter formulas into cells. You may enter these formulas by two methods, typing or pointing.

■ 1-2-3 has built-in functions. Functions are used in the worksheet the same way as formulas. All functions start with the @ symbol.

Quick Check: Building a Spreadsheet

1. What are the types of cell entries that 1-2-3 allows?

2. What are the label prefixes used in 1-2-3?

3. Name two ways that you may edit a cell entry after you have pressed [Enter]?

4. Write the formula to subtract the cell contents of E5 from the cell contents of D5 and place the result in cell F5.

5. How could you sum the contents of cells A6 through A10 and store the result in A12 using the @SUM function?

Using the Command Menu

Commands are the instructions you give to perform a variety of tasks from formatting and graphing data to saving and retrieving spreadsheets.

The Command Menu presents the command alternatives to you. To display this menu type a slash [/]. You have used the File Save (/FS) and File Retrieve (/FR) command already in this course. The entire first level of the command menu follows:

Command	Action
Worksheet	Commands that affect the entire worksheet.
Range	Commands that affect a specific section of the worksheet.
Copy	Copies a range to another area of the worksheet.
Move	Moves a range to another area of the worksheet.

File	Saves and retrieves files (worksheets).
Print	Prints worksheets.
Graph	Enters the graph menu.
Data	Enters the data management menu.
System	Allows accessing DOS from Lotus.
Quit	Exits the spreadsheet segment of Lotus.

As you move through the Lotus command menu, you will notice that on the third line of the control panel is an explanation or submenu of that particular command.

Getting Help from the Screen

The 1-2-3 display area is divided into two parts:

- The control panel at the top of the screen
- The spreadsheet area

The Control Panel

The area above the reverse video border is the control panel. This area has three lines. The first line contains all the information about the current cell:

Current cell	The cell where the 1-2-3 pointer is currently located.
Display format	Tells what format the cell contents are displaying.
Cell contents	

The second line of the control panel displays either the command menu or worksheet data that is being entered or edited.

The third line contains explanations of the current command menu item. When you move the pointer from one item to the next in a command menu the explanation on the third line will change. If you are not in this command menu, the third line will be blank.

Modes

There are several modes in 1-2-3, one of which is always in effect. The mode indicator is highlighted in the upper right corner of the screen and will show the current mode. The following is a list of mode indicators:

Mode	Explanation
Ready	1-2-3 is ready to do your bidding.
Value	A number or formula is being entered.
Label	A label is being entered.
Point	Moving the pointer to indicate a cell or a range.
Menu	Selecting a menu choice.
Edit	A cell entry is being edited.
Help	On-line help facility is being used.
Wait	1-2-3 is busy and cannot respond to commands.
Find	Data Query Find operation is in progress.
Error	Something is wrong. Press [Esc] or [Return].

Special Key Indicators

Whenever a special key is used or a circular reference occurs, an indicator is displayed at the bottom of the screen.

Indicators	Explanation
Lock Key	There are three lock keys: number lock, caps lock, and scroll lock.
End	The [End] key has been pressed.
Calc	Manual recalculation is set.
Circ	A circular reference has been found.

Error Message Location

When an error occurs, the Error mode indicator blinks in the top right corner of the screen, and a message appears in the bottom left corner of the screen. To clear the error and get back to the Ready mode you must hit [Esc] or [Return]. If you do not press one of those keys, the message will not be cleared. Press [Help] [F1] for an explanation and remedy for the error or consult the Lotus Reference Manual.

Getting Help from the Program [F1]

Lotus 1-2-3 contains over 200 on-line help screens. By pressing [F1], 1-2-3 suspends the current operation and gives you access to the Help screen. The following information is displayed.

- Instructions and procedures relevant to current operations.

- A list of related topics. You simply move your cursor to another topic and press [RETURN].

- Next step options, or a submenu option may be displayed in the menu area at the bottom of the screen.

Key	Action
[Backspace]	Returns to previous HELP screen.
[Esc]	Exits the HELP mode and returns to the worksheet.

Activity 2-4: Getting On-line Help

Task	Procedure
Invoke the on-line Help facility.	Press [F1].
Go to "How to Use Help."	Move [right arrow →] until "How to Use Help" is highlighted [R].
Use the "Help Index."	Select "Help Index" by moving to it with the right arrow and [R].
Select "Moving the Cell Pointer."	Using the arrow keys and [R] to select.
Return to worksheet.	Press [Esc].

On Your Own: Using Prefixes

Task

1. Try entering dates into a blank area of the spreadsheet as follows:

   12/12/89

   12-12-89

   What happens. Why? How would you fix it?

2. Try entering the following:

   1990 Budget

   What happens? How would you fix it?

3. Try entering:

   B3+B4+B5

   What happens? How would you fix it?

Summary: Getting Help

■ 1-2-3 contains a command menu that allows you to instruct 1-2-3 to perform a variety of tasks. You invoke this command menu by typing a [/].

■ The 1-2-3 display area is divided into the control panel and the spreadsheet area. The control panel contains all the information about the current cell or displays the command menu.

■ There are several modes in 1-2-3 which are indicated on the upper right corner of the screen. These modes give you information on your current status.

■ There are special keys in 1-2-3 that are displayed in the lower right hand corner of the screen. These indicators will tell you if certain keys are in effect, such as the [Caps Lock] key.

■ Error messages appear at the bottom left corner of the screen.

■ 1-2-3 has an on-line help facility. By pressing [F1], you are invoking this feature.

Quick Check: Getting Help

1. What is the control panel? What information does it contain?

2. What is meant by "current cell"?

3. What are some of the modes in 1-2-3, and what do they indicate?

4. How does one clear an error in 1-2-3 and get back to the Ready mode?

5. How does one invoke the 1-2-3 Help facility?

6. How is the command menu invoked?

Case Study #1: A Personal Budget

Create your own personal budget. Allow an area for income and an area where you will list at least five expenses. Total the expenses and subtract this total from your gross income giving you your net income. Save your worksheet as PERSBUDG.

UNIT·3·

Forecasting with Lotus

Overview:

In this module you will expand the budgetary spreadsheet you created in the last module to include four quarters of actual data. 1-2-3's capabilities for flexible copying of ranges will be used to ease these tasks. The power of the electronic spreadsheet to facilitate "what-if" thinking will also be explored in this module. Factors such as salary increases and inflation rates will be examined by creating special cells (input cells) for these values and basing any related cells in the rest of the spreadsheet on them. Before making changes in your spreadsheet, various ways of backing up files and ranges will be considered.

Skills:

Making backups

Inserting new rows

Copying labels and values

Setting up input cells

Copying formulas

Absolute and relative references

Asking what-if questions

Completed Model

	A	B	C	D	E	F	G
6		Current					
7		Average		Projected Quarterly Expenses			
8		Quarterly					
9	Item	Expenses	1	2	3	4	Total
10							
11	Salaries	85000	87125	89303.12	91535.70	93824.09	361787.9
12	Benefits	11900	12197.5	12502.43	12814.99	13135.37	50650.30
13	Equipment	22500	22612.5	22725.56	22839.19	22953.38	91130.63
14	Service	2250	2261.25	2272.556	2283.919	2295.338	9113.063
15	Software	1800	1809	1818.045	1827.135	1836.270	7290.451
16	Supplies	6500	6630	6762.6	6897.852	7035.809	27326.26
17	Rent	15000	15300	15606	15918.12	16236.48	63060.60
18	Utilities	5500	5610	5722.2	5836.644	5953.376	23122.22
19	Travel	4250	4335	4421.7	4510.134	4600.336	17867.17
20							
21	Totals	154700	157880.2	161134.2	164463.6	167870.4	651348.6

Making Backups

An important habit to establish when using any computer system is to make copies of your software and data. Copying data or programs is called "backing up" those data or programs. Backing up your spreadsheets can save hours of redesigning and retyping if a disk is damaged or erased, and provides a safe way to make modifications and extensions in an existing spreadsheet.

Selected files (spreadsheets) or an entire disk can be copied by using the Lotus Access System or the DOS Copy utility.

A simple way to save a copy of a spreadsheet while you are working in 1-2-3 is to save it using the FILE SAVE (/FS) command. You can also save the spreadsheet under a different name on the same data disk, or under the same name on a different data disk. In the following activity you will load the spreadsheet you built in the last module and save it to another name on the same data disk. You will then have two versions of the spreadsheet, one of which you can experiment with while maintaining an original version if your experimental modifications do not work out.

Activity 3-1: Creating a Backup Copy of a Spreadsheet

		Procedure
Task	Cell Location	Enter
Load the EXPENSE1 spreadsheet.		/FR EXPENSE1 [R]
Save under another name.		/FS EXPTEMP [R]
Check to see if it was saved.		/FLW
Return to the spreadsheet.		[Ctrl] [Break]

Note: Never enter spaces in Lotus commands. Press the Enter or Return key only when you see [R] in the instructions. Instructions for entering keystrokes may be on more than one line, or may contain spaces to make them easier to read. DO NOT ENTER SPACES.

Inserting a New Row

In the activity that follows you will add a new row for software expenses in the spreadsheet.

The steps for adding a new row are:

- Insert blank rows using /WORKSHEET INSERT ROW (rows are inserted above the specified row).
- Type the new data into the blank rows.

Activity 3-2: Inserting a New Row

	Procedure	
Task	Cell Location	Enter
Insert a new row above Supplies.	A15	/WIR [R]
Add the new item (Software).	A15	Software [R]
Add the average quarterly expense.	B15	1800 [R]

Planning for Forecasting

In your spreadsheet, you have a set of average quarterly expenses from the previous year. You wish to project quarterly expenses for various salary increases, equipment increases, and inflation factors. Some questions you wish to answer are:

1. What will be the third quarter salary expenses if salaries are increased 2.5% per quarter?

2. What if salaries are increased 1.5% per quarter?

3. What will expenses for rent and utilities be if you experience a 2% per quarter inflation rate?

4. What will these expenses be if inflation is 1.25% per quarter?

To answer questions like these you can enter individual formulas for each category of expense in each quarter, using the rate of increase for each formula.

Category	Formula
Salary	Salary * 1.025
Benefits	Benefits * 1.025

To determine the effect on salary of different percent increases, you could rewrite the formula and observe the results for each increase in question.

Lotus allows you to establish a single cell, called an *input cell*, to reference that cell in the formulas in the individual cells, and finally to copy these cells across a cell range. Simply changing the value in the input cell allows you to see the effects of different salary increases.

In the following activities, you will:

- Practice copying cells and cell ranges.
- Create input cells.
- Construct formulas referencing these cells.
- Copy these formulas across the spreadsheet.

The COPY Command

The COPY command is essential in making spreadsheet projections. You can create new cell entries by copying existing cells, and, more importantly, by copying formulas. Since formulas are built relative to their spreadsheet position, copies of these formulas will reflect the new position automatically.

Relative Copying

In the sample spreadsheet below, the @SUM function was copied to the two adjoining columns. Notice that the new functions reflect the sum relative to the position in which the function (or formula) is copied. If copies were absolute, then the same formula, @SUM(B5..B7) would be copied to the remaining columns, producing an incorrect result.

SAMPLE SPREADSHEET:

	A	B	C	D
1		Automobile Expenses		
2				
3	Item	Jan	Feb	Mar
4				
5	Gasoline	45.00	53.00	42.00
6	Payment	281.00	281.00	281.00
7	Service	0.00	0.00	145.50
8				
9	Total	@SUM(B5..B7)	@SUM(C5..C7)	@SUM(D5..D7)

Cell ranges can be copied in any of the following ways:

From	To
Single cell	Single cell
Single cell	Cell range
Cell range	Cell range

The COPY command appears on the main 1-2-3 menu and is invoked by typing /C.

There are two ranges to be specified in the COPY command:

- Range to copy FROM:
- Range to copy TO:

Although you can copy a cell or cell range with the cell pointer anyplace on the spreadsheet, it is much easier to place the cell pointer on the cell to be copied before invoking the COPY command. 1-2-3 will propose the current cell as the one to copy from and you can simply press [Return] to confirm the response.

Absolute Copying

There are cases where you do not want 1-2-3 to automatically adjust a cell reference in a formula you are copying. In a previous activity you set up input cells for your spreadsheet. The values for increases were to remain constant for each quarter; you do not want 1-2-3 to adjust F1 to G1 as you copy any formula containing F1 one cell to the right. The $ prefixes tell 1-2-3 to copy that cell exactly as is, that is, absolutely.

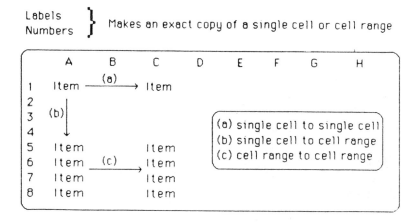

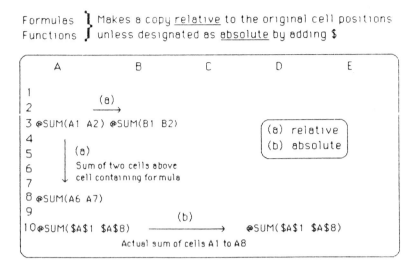

Formulas ⎤ Makes a copy <u>relative</u> to the original cell positions
Functions ⎦ unless designated as <u>absolute</u> by adding $

Activity 3-3: Setting Up Input Cells

In the activities that follow you will create input cells for salary increases, equipment cost increases, and inflation based on the previous year's average quarterly expenses and the input cells' values.

	Procedure	
Task	**Cell Location**	**Enter**
Enter the input cell labels.	D1	Salary: [R]
	D2	Inflation: [R]
	D3	Equipment: [R]
Enter the projected increases.	F1	.025 [R]
	F2	.02 [R]
	F3	.005 [R]
Save the spreadsheet under the name EXPENSE2.		/FS EXPENSE2 [R]

Compare your spreadsheet to the following one.

Spreadsheet Reflecting Input Cells

	A	B	C	D	E	F	G
1	Name:	Jane Doe		Salary:		0.025	
2	Date:	<today's date>		Inflation:		0.02	
3	Subject:	Budget Projection		Equipment:		0.005	
4							
5							
6		Current					
7		Average		Projected Quarterly Expenses			
8		Quarterly					
9	Item	Expenses	1	2	3	4	Total
10							
11	Salaries	85000					
12	Benefits	11900					
13	Equipment	22500					
14	Service	2250					
15	Software	1800					
16	Supplies	6500					
17	Rent	15000					
18	Utilities	5500					
19	Travel	4250					
20							
21	Total	154700					

Activity 3-4: Formulas for First Quarter Expenses

You will now enter the formulas for the first quarter. Recall that a 2% increase can be represented by multiplying the base amount by 1.02 (102%). Since the cell F1 contains the value for salary increase, you can use (1+F1) to multiply the previous salary amount.

Because 1-2-3 automatically adjusts cell labels when copying formulas, you must inform 1-2-3 to use the same value (F1) each time, no matter where the F1 appears in the spreadsheet. You indicate an absolute cell reference by using $ prefixes for the column and row. For example, $F$1 represents the value in F1 no matter where you copy any formula which references F1. You will have more practice copying formulas in a later activity.

		Procedure	
Task		**Cell Location**	**Enter**
Enter the formula for the salary increase for the first quarter.		C11	+B11*(1+$F$1)[R]
Copy the formula to Benefits.		C11	/C[R]C12[R]
Enter the formula for Equipment.		C13	+B13*(1+$F$3)[R]
Copy the formula to Service and Software.		C13	/C[R]C14..C15[R]
Enter the formula for Office Supplies.		C16	+B16*(1+$F$2)[R]
Copy the formula to Rent, Utilities, and Travel.		C16	/C[R]C17..C19[R]
Replace EXPENSE2.			/FS[R]R

Compare your spreadsheet to the one below.

Spreadsheet Reflecting Formulas for Making Projections

	A	B	C	D	E	F	G
1	Name:	Jane Doe		Salary:		0.025	
2	Date:	<today's date>		Inflation:		0.02	
3	Subject:	Budget Projection		Equipment:		0.005	
4							
5							
6		Current					
7		Average		Projected Quarterly Expenses			
8		Quarterly					
9	Item	Expenses	1	2	3	4	Total
10							
11	Salaries	85000	87125				
12	Benefits	11900	12197.5				
13	Equipment	22500	22612.5				
14	Service	2250	2261.25				
15	Software	1800	1809				
16	Supplies	6500	6630				
17	Rent	15000	15300				
18	Utilities	5500	5610				
19	Travel	4250	4335				
20							
21	Total	154700					

Activity 3-5: Copying Formulas

In the following activity you will use the COPY command to complete the spreadsheet for the remaining three quarters. You may use typing or pointing to identify cell ranges.

	Procedure	
Task	Cell Location	Enter
Copy Salaries formula.	C11	/C[R] D11..F11[R]
Copy Benefits formula.	C12	/C[R] D12..F12[R]

You could go on copying each formula to the adjacent range of cells. However, in previous exercises, you learned that cell ranges as well as individual cells could be copied. To save you many keystrokes and much time, you will copy the remaining formulas with one copy command.

Copy all formulas from C13..C19 to the adjacent range, D13..F19.	C13	/C C13..C19[R] D13..F19[R]
Copy the @SUM function in the Total cell to the Total cells for each quarter.	B21	/C[R] C21..F21[R]

Challenge

Create an @SUM function in
G11 to sum Salaries for the 4
quarters of 1986.

Copy the formula down to
G19.

Copy the formula in F21 to
G21.

Replace EXPENSE2.   /FS[R]R

Compare your spreadsheet to the following one.

Spreadsheet Reflecting Copied Formulas

	A	B	C	D	E	F	G
1	Name:	Jane Doe		Salary:		0.025	
2	Date:	<today's date>		Inflation:		0.02	
3	Subject:	Budget Projection		Equipment:		0.005	
4							
5							
6		Current					
7		Average		Projected Quarterly Expenses			
8		Quarterly					
9	Item	Expenses	1	2	3	4	Total
10							
11	Salaries	85000	87125	89303.12	91535.70	93824.09	361787.9
12	Benefits	11900	12197.5	12502.43	12814.99	13135.37	50650.30
13	Equipment	22500	22612.5	22725.56	22839.19	22953.38	91130.63
14	Service	2250	2261.25	2272.556	2283.919	2295.338	9113.063
15	Software	1800	1809	1818.045	1827.135	1836.270	7290.451
16	Supplies	6500	6630	6762.6	6897.852	7035.809	27326.26
17	Rent	15000	15300	15606	15918.12	16236.48	63060.60
18	Utilities	5500	5610	5722.2	5836.644	5953.376	23122.22
19	Travel	4250	4335	4421.7	4510.134	4600.336	17867.17
20							
21	Total	154700	157880.2	161134.2	164463.6	167870.4	651348.6

Asking What-If Questions

You have a spreadsheet which reflects data for salary increases of 2.5% per quarter, an inflation rate of 2% per quarter, and equipment cost increases of 0.5% per quarter. To examine the effects of other rates of increase you can simply enter different values in the input cells and watch all related values on the spreadsheet be immediately updated. Systematically varying these values to observe their effects on the entire budget is a powerful technique for planning and decision making. 1-2-3 facilitates the ease of asking and answering "what-if" questions.

Activity 3-6: What-If Questions

In the following activity, you will change the rates of increase to answer what-if questions.

	Procedure	
Task	Cell Location	Enter
What is the third quarter salary if increases of 3% are given?	F1	.03[R]

Observe new value in E11.

What is rent for the fourth quarter if the inflation rate is 3.5% per quarter?	F2	.035[R]

If Total Annual Salaries must be kept below 400,000, what is the maximum possible quarterly increase?

If Total Annual Equipment expenditures must be kept below 90,000, what is the maximum quarterly increase?

Use your spreadsheet to answer your own what-if questions.

Save your spreadsheet.   /FS[R]R

On Your Own: Asking What-If Questions

Task

Retrieve the PERSBUDG file you made in Case Study #1.

Suppose you expect to make more money next year, but expenses will probably increase faster. Start another column for next year. Project your income increasing by 7% and your expenses increasing by 10%.

Again sum your expenses and subtract the total from your income.

Summary: Forecasting with Lotus

- It is important to make backups of your files and disks.

- Disks can be backed up using the Lotus Access System or DOS utilities.

- Files (spreadsheets) or ranges can be backed up by saving them under different names on the same disk or the same name on different disks.

- Using input cells facilitates forecasting with 1-2-3.

- The COPY command allows copying of ranges to other ranges.

- The COPY command copies formulas in relative fashion unless specifically told to use absolute references.

- Absolute references are indicated by $ prefixes in the column and/or row cell labels.

- One of the most powerful uses of 1-2-3 is to facilitate the asking and answering of what-if questions.

Quick Check: Forecasting with Lotus

1. What cell should be changed to see the effects of a 1% inflation rate?

2. Give an example of a what-if question this spreadsheet could not answer as it now stands.

3. What other factors could be built into the spreadsheet by adding other input cells?

4. Assume a new category, Entertainment, was added to the spreadsheet in A20.

   a. What command would add the new row?

   b. What formula would you put in C20?

   c. In copying C20 to D20..F20 would the $F$2 be copied relatively or absolutely?

   d. In copying C20 to D20..F20 would the B20 be copied relatively or absolutely?

5. How would you get a listing of all of your worksheet filenames on disk? Specify the command.

UNIT·4·

Formatting Spreadsheets

Overview: Once all data has been entered into a spreadsheet,
you can format both the numeric and label entries
allowing for clearer interpretation and enhanced
appearance. Spreadsheets can also be globally
formatted or formatted by single cell prior to
entering data or at any time during the data entry
process. Choose the method that best suits your own
work style.

Skills: Global formatting

Local formatting

Formatting labels

Formatting numeric entries

Altering column width

Locking titles

Generating new data

Completed Model

	A	B	C	D	E	F
1	Name:	Jane Doe		Salary:		2.50%
2	Date:	<today's date>		Inflation:		2.00%
3	Subject:	Budget Projection		Equipment:		0.50%
4						
5	--					
6		Current				
7		Average		Projected Quarterly Expenses		
8		Quarterly	---			
9	Item	Expenses	1	2	3	4
10	--					
11	Salaries	85,000.00	87,125.00	89,303.13	91,535.70	93,824.10
12	Benefits	11,900.00	12,197.50	12,502.44	12,815.00	13,135.37
13	Equipment	22,500.00	22,612.50	22,725.56	22,839.19	22,953.39
14	Service	2,250.00	2,261.25	2,272.56	2,283.92	2,295.34
15	Software	1,800.00	1,809.00	1,818.05	1,827.14	1,836.27
16	Supplies	6,500.00	6,630.00	6,762.60	6,897.85	7,035.81
17	Rent	15,000.00	15,300.00	15,606.00	15,918.12	16,236.48
18	Utilities	5,500.00	5,610.00	5,722.20	5,836.64	5,953.38
19	Travel	4,250.00	4,335.00	4,421.70	4,510.13	4,600.34
20						
21	Total	$154,700.00	$157,880.25	$161,134.23	$164,463.70	$167,870.47

The FORMAT Command

Formatting a cell or a range of cells allows you to control how cell contents are displayed. 1-2-3 provides you with ten different format options through the menu, which is invoked with a slash (/). Selections are made either by typing the first letter of the command or by highlighting it and pressing [R]. A format option may be applied to the entire worksheet or specific cell range.

Area to Format	Command
Entire worksheet	WORKSHEET GLOBAL FORMAT (/WGF)
Specific cell range	RANGE FORMAT (/RF)

The ten formatting options, whether global or local, are as follows:

Format	**Explanation**
General	This is the default setting for 1-2-3. All labels are left-justified, all numbers right-justified.
Fixed	The value is expressed with a fixed number of decimal places. You may specify up to fifteen decimal places.
Scientific	The number is expressed in exponential notation. For example, the number 10 is expressed as 1.00E+01.
Currency	Each number is preceded by a dollar sign, and thousands are separated by a comma. Negative numbers appear in parentheses. You may have up to fifteen decimal places.
Comma	Same as currency format except that no dollar signs are displayed.
+/-	Integer portion of number displayed in horizontal graph format. A + for positive values and a - for negative values and a . for zero values. For example, the number 5 would produce the result, '+++++'.
Percent	The value is represented as a value multiplied by 100. The value is followed by a percent % sign.
Text	The formulas are represented rather than their values. For example, @SUM(A2..A5) would appear rather than the value that this function yields. Numbers are represented in the General Format.
Date	The numeric representation of the date is displayed in one of five formats:

DD-MMM-YY	1-Jan-88
DD-MMM	1-Jan
MMM-YY	Jan-88
Long Intn'l	01/01/88
Short Intn'l	01/01

A Time format is also available in this menu, and it has four formats available in a submenu.

| Hidden | The display is hidden. |

In addition, the local (Range format) menu has a feature called Reset, which returns the current column to the default (General) format.

Tips for Formatting Spreadsheets

- If the value you want to display is too large for the column width, a series of asterisks (*********) will appear across the cell instead of the value. The best way to handle this is to adjust the column width and experiment with various format options until you get the appearance you want.

- Another point to remember when formatting is that 1-2-3 stores the number in the form that it is entered, not in the format in which it appears in the worksheet. Therefore, a number that is entered as 3.4567 would be stored exactly as entered. However, if you were to format this using the currency option with two decimal places, it would be displayed as $3.46. No change is made to the original entry.

Formatting the Entire Worksheet

The WORKSHEET GLOBAL FORMAT command allows you to set the format for the entire worksheet. The default setting is the General format as described previously.

Using the WORKSHEET GLOBAL FORMAT command does not affect other cell ranges that have been formatted with the RANGE FORMAT command. For example, if you have one column of your worksheet formatted using the Fixed option, invoking the WORKSHEET GLOBAL FORMAT CURRENCY command will change all existing values to currency except those which were previously set with the RANGE FORMAT FIXED command.

Formatting Specific Ranges

You can determine the format for each cell by moving the cursor to a formatted cell. The format designation appears in the upper left-hand corner of the screen. The first character is the format option and the number of decimal places is shown. Both are enclosed in parentheses.

Examples of Format Indicators

Format	Format Indicator
Fixed format (zero/no decimal places)	(F0)
Currency format (2 decimal places)	(C2)
Date formats	(D1)
	(D2)
	(D3)

Formatting Labels

The default setting for all text or label entries is left justified. The command WORKSHEET GLOBAL LABEL-PREFIX can be used to format the text alignment of an entire worksheet. After issuing this command, you are given the option of Left, Right, or Center. By choosing any of these three all text data will be aligned accordingly.

It is important to realize that the WORKSHEET GLOBAL LABEL-PREFIX command does not realign any previously aligned entries. For example, if you have centered a particular row of entries the WORK-SHEET GLOBAL LABEL-PREFIX command does not alter that row.

Previously entered text can be realigned by either editing the original entry or issuing the RANGE LABEL command. The RANGE LABEL command allows you to specify left, right, or center alignment for a range of cells. You may not issue the RANGE LABEL command before you enter any data.

Changing the Column Width

The initial global column width setting is nine characters. This default setting can be altered by using the WORKSHEET GLOBAL COLUMN-WIDTH command. Once the command is entered you may then increase or decrease the column width by using the right or left arrows, or by typing in the desired width.

Individual column widths may be set using the same procedure with the WORKSHEET COLUMN SET-WIDTH command. The settings established using the this command are not overridden when a WORK-SHEET GLOBAL COLUMN-WIDTH command is issued, unless you have previously restored those settings to the default by placing the cursor in the column you wish to reset, and issuing the WORKSHEET COLUMN RESET-WIDTH command.

Tips for Setting Column Width

- Column width settings range from 1 to 240 characters.

- Text, values, or formulas can extend beyond the column width setting. If no information is entered in the cells to the right of the entry, the full cell entry is displayed on the screen. However, if information is entered in the adjacent cell, the display of the initial cell is truncated. Spaces entered with the spacebar count as information.

- If text has been entered using the centering label prefix (^), the text will still be centered as the column width increases.

- Remember that numbers cannot be changed from the default right justification (using label prefixes) without changing them from values to labels. If that is done, they will not be calculated.

- Any new column inserted will have the global column width setting.

Activity 4-1:   Formatting the Spreadsheet

		Procedure	
Task		Cell Location	Enter
Retrieve worksheet EXPENSE2.			/FR EXPENSE2 [R]
Expand all column widths (global) to 12 places.			/WGC12 [R]
Replace contents of B2 with the Date function.		B2	@DATE(yy,mm,dd) [R]
Change format to Date.		B2	/RFD
Select 1 (DD-MMM-YY) format for B2.			[R] [R]
Change format of cells in F1..F3 to percent with 2 decimal places.		F1 F3	/RFP [R] [R]

		Procedure	
Task		**Cell Location**	**Enter**
Change format of cells in		B11	/RF, [R]
B11..F19 , (Comma) with 2		B19	
decimal places.		F19	[R]
Change format of cells in			
B21..F21 to Currency with 2		B21	/RFC [R]
decimal places.		F21	[R]
Enter repeating labels, --------,		A5	\-[R]
in A5, C8, and A10, and copy			/C [R] B5..F5 [R]
across, to "draw" lines on the		C8	\-[R]
spreadsheet.			/C [R] D8..F8 [R]
		A10	\-[R]
			/C [R] B10..F10 [R]
Save worksheet as EXPENSE3.			/FS EXPENSE3 [R]

Compare your spreadsheet with the one below.

Spreadsheet Reflecting Formatting Changes

		Current		Projected Quarterly Expenses		
6		Current				
7		Average		Projected Quarterly Expenses		
8		Quarterly				
9	Item	Expenses	1	2	3	4
10						
11	Salaries	85,000.00	87,125.00	89,303.13	91,535.70	93,824.10
12	Benefits	11,900.00	12,197.50	12,502.44	12,815.00	13,135.37
13	Equipment	22,500.00	22,612.50	22,725.56	22,839.19	22,953.39
14	Service	2,250.00	2,261.25	2,272.56	2,283.92	2,295.34
15	Software	1,800.00	1,809.00	1,818.05	1,827.14	1,836.27
16	Supplies	6,500.00	6,630.00	6,762.60	6,897.85	7,035.81
17	Rent	15,000.00	15,300.00	15,606.00	15,918.12	16,236.48
18	Utilities	5,500.00	5.610.00	5,722.20	5,836.64	5,953.38
19	Travel	4,250.00	4,335.00	4,421.70	4,510.13	4,600.34
20						
21	Total	$154,700.00	$157,880.25	$161,134.23	$164,463.70	$167,870.47

Fixing Titles

You have several options available to you that permit you to view two or more parts of a worksheet simultaneously. You may need these options if you are doing "what-if" analysis, and the input area is far from the area where the results are being shown.

WORKSHEET TITLES Command

This command allows you to fix the display of specified rows or columns at the top and/or left of the screen. You would use the WORKSHEET TITLES command to fix column and/or row headings when entering data. Since the cursor cannot be moved into areas that have been fixed with this command, you can use this command to protect previously entered data.

When you enter the command the following menu appears:

Both   Horizontal   Vertical   Clear

Command	Explanation
Both	Freezes the rows above and the columns to the left of the cell pointer.
Horizontal	Means the rows on the screen above the cell pointer are frozen. They will stay in position when you scroll up and down.
Vertical	Means the columns to the left of the cell pointer are frozen. They will move only when you scroll up and down but not when you move left and right.
Clear	Unlocks any previously set worksheet titles.

Once the WORKSHEET TITLES command has been invoked, you cannot move the pointer into the protected area. The one exception is through the use of the [F5] [Go To] function key. You may press [F5] and then by either typing a cell location or by pointing to a cell you may change these protected cells.

WORKSHEET WINDOW Command

Using windows is another way of viewing two parts of the spreadsheet at the same time. WORKSHEET WINDOW permits the choice of having a HORIZONTAL or VERTICAL screen split. The cursor should be positioned before invoking the command, as the current row (if HORIZONTAL is chosen) or current column (if VERTICAL is chosen) becomes the first row or column in the second window.

[F6] is used to move the cell pointer between windows. The cell pointer can be moved anywhere in the spreadsheet, and although there is only one cell pointer, there are two current cells, one in each window.

SYNC and UNSYNC are available in the menu. SYNC is the default, linking the current cells and permitting BOTH screens to move together. UNSYNC makes the current cells independent, so that when one window moves, the other does not adjust.

CLEAR returns to a single window.

Activity 4-2: Fixing Titles

| | Procedure | |
Task	Cell Location	Enter
Retrieve EXPENSE3.		/FR EXPENSE3 [R]
Lock both horizontal and vertical titles.	B11	/WTB
Scroll through the spreadsheet.		
Try to edit a title.		
Unlock titles.		/WTC

Note that you once again can move the cell pointer into the title area.

Activity 4-3: Comparative Statistics

In the following activity, you will generate the average projected expenses for each category and a column displaying the difference between the current year's average and the projected average. You will freeze the column containing the current averages to compare the generated statistics.

	Procedure	
Task	Cell Location	Enter
Load the completed version of EXPENSE3.		/FREXPENSES3 [R]
Place the cursor anywhere in column C and freeze the screen at column B.	C	/WTV
Move the cursor to the right to bring column G (Totals) next to B.		
Enter titles for "Projected Average" and "Difference."	H8	Projected [R]
	H9	Average [R]
	I9	Difference [R]
Construct a formula in H11 to produce a quarterly average.	H11	+G11/4 [R]
Copy the formula down to H21; erase H20 to prevent zeros.	H11	/C [R]
		H12..H21 [R]
	H20	/RE [R]
Format as in column G.	H11	/RF, [R]
		H11..H19 [R]
	H21	/RFC [R] [R]

Challenge

Generate a column in I to display the difference between the quarterly averages. Enter a formula in I11, copy the formula down the column, and format as desired.

Replace the old version of EXPENSE3.		/FS[R]R

Compare your spreadsheet with the following one.

Spreadsheet Reflecting Comparative Statistics

	A	B	G	H	I
4					
5		-----	-----	-----	-----
6		Current			
7		Average			
8		Quarterly		Projected	
9	Item	Expenses	Total	Average	Difference
10		-----	-----	-----	-----
11	Salaries	85,000.00	361,787.92	90,446.98	5,446.98
12	Benefits	11,900.00	50,650.31	12,662.58	762.58
13	Equipment	22,500.00	91,130.64	22,782.66	282.66
14	Service	2,250.00	9,113.06	2,278.27	28.27
15	Software	1,800.00	7,290.45	1,822.61	22.61
16	Supplies	6,500.00	27,326.26	6,831.57	331.57
17	Rent	15,000.00	63,060.60	15,765.15	765.15
18	Utilities	5,500.00	23,122.22	5,780.56	280.56
19	Travel	4,250.00	17,867.17	4,466.79	216.79
20					
21	Total	$154,700.00	$651,348.64	$162,837.16	$8,137.16
22					
23					

On Your Own: Using Formats and Formulas

Task

1. Retrieve your personal budget file.

2. Format it to Comma with 2 decimal places. It may be necessary to make the column width larger.

3. Set up a column comparing the current year and next year's projected figures.

4. When costs rise faster than income, a deficit may occur. If you find that your total expenses will be more than your total income next year, see what percentage decrease in spending is needed to bring you within your income. Test it on next year's expenses.

Summary: Formatting Spreadsheets

■ There are ten formatting options in 1-2-3: General, Fixed, Scientific, Currency, Comma, +/-, Percent, Text, Date, and Hidden.

■ You may format the entire worksheet with the WORKSHEET GLOBAL FORMAT command or a specific range of cells with the RANGE FORMAT command.

■ You may format labels globally by using the WORKSHEET GLOBAL LABEL-PREFIX command or locally with the RANGE LABEL command.

■ Changing column widths is accomplished globally using the WORKSHEET GLOBAL COLUMN-WIDTH command or on individual columns using the WORKSHEET COLUMN SET-WIDTH command.

■ You may lock titles into place using the WORKSHEET TITLES command or you may split the worksheet into windows using the WORKSHEET WINDOW command.

Quick Check: Formatting Spreadsheets

1. What Format command will display formulas rather than the values that these formulas represent?

2. What will happen if the value you want to display is too large for the column width?

3. What command allows you to format the entire worksheet?

4. What command allows you to center a range of labels? Write the command if the range is A3..F3.

5. What is the default setting of label entries?

6. What is the command to globally change column widths to 12 characters?

7. What is the command that will allow you to split a worksheet into two vertical windows?

8. What does the SYNC option mean in windowing?

Case Study #2: Lease versus Buy Option

You are responsible for a five-year plan to acquire and maintain a computer system for your office. The system consists of a number of CPU's, monochrome and/or color monitors, hard-disk drives, printers, software, and a service contract for the system. There are two options for you to consider:

1. Buy Option: Total amount is due at purchase time. You are also responsible for carrying a service contract which is 15% of the original purchase price for each of the five years.

2. Lease Option: The cost of leasing is 35% of the total purchase price for each of the five years with all maintenance, service, and parts included in the leasing cost. At the end of the lease period, you can purchase the equipment for 10% of the original sales price.

Items	Unit Cost	Units Needed
CPU	2250	5
Monochrome mon.	110	2
Color monitor	425	3
Hard disk (40Mb)	1100	1
Printer (laser)	1650	1
Printer (dot)	400	4
Software	1900	5

Determine the annual cash outflow for each of the five years under each option. Determine the total cash outflow. Assume your spreadsheet is for presentation; therefore, you must consider layout, titles, etc.

Challenge

How would you set up an input cell to evaluate lease options from other companies with different annual rates and final purchase prices? Are there other factors to consider in determining whether to lease or buy?

Save your spreadsheet as PLAN.   /FS PLAN[R]

UNIT·5·

Displaying Spreadsheet Data

Overview: Producing hard copy of worksheets is mandatory and easily accomplished through the Lotus PRINT command. A whole range of options exists for printing both selected ranges and the entire work-sheet.

In addition, worksheet data can be graphically displayed using the Lotus GRAPH command, and, once graphs are created and saved, printed using the PRINTGRAPH utility selected from the Lotus Access Menu. Although Lotus 1-2-3 is capable of efficiently producing graphic representation of spreadsheet data, its graphs do not meet the current state-of-the-art in computer graphics. In this unit you will explore what is possible within Lotus to enhance the basic graphs and charts, and what possibilities exist in third party software for graphic enhancement.

Skills:
Exploring the PRINT options

Printing ranges

Sending setup strings to the printer

Printing to disk

Exploring the GRAPH options

Creating a PIE and BAR graph

Printing graphs using PRINTGRAPH

Exploring Lotus graphing options

Exploring third party Lotus-compatible graphic software

The PRINT Command

Lotus 1-2-3 gives you many options when printing your spreadsheet. You have a choice as to whether you would like to print directly to your printer, create a file to be printed at a later date, or print headers and footers with page numbers. If you prefer, you can just use the system defaults without selecting any other options.

When the /PRINT command is entered, two choices are displayed:

- Printer   Specifications that follow go directly to the printer.
- File   Stores the output in a file to be printed at a later time. Use the command /PRINT FILE if your system does not support a printer, or if you are transferring the data to other software or program.

Regardless of what option you choose, the following Print menu is displayed:

Range Line Page Options Clear Align Go Quit

If you are using a *stand-alone* (nonnetwork) system, the sequence of commands when printing are:

    /PRINT
    PRINTER or FILE
    RANGE
    GO

If you are using a networked system, see your technical support person for any changes in the print procedure.

Selecting a Print Range

When you enter /PRINT PRINTER RANGE, the most recently entered range is highlighted. You may enter a range by pointing to the cell, entering the cell address, or entering a range name. You must press the Enter key [R] after specifying the range. 1-2-3 then returns you to the Print menu.

If the specified range exceeds the right margin setting, 1-2-3 splits the data range at the margin setting and prints the remaining data immediately below the first.

Go and Quit

When /PRINT PRINTER GO is entered, 1-2-3 will print the specified range. Printing can be stopped by pressing the [CTRL] and [BREAK] key at the same time. 1-2-3 will return you to the Print menu when printing is completed.

To exit the Print menu enter the QUIT command or press the [ESC] key.

Printer Options

The printer options choice allows you to design customized reports. When /PRINT PRINTER OPTIONS is entered the following menu is displayed:

Header Footer Margins Borders Setup Page-length Other Quit

Option	Explanation
Header/Footer ·	Allows an extra line of text to be printed at the top(header) or the bottom(footer) of each page.
Margins	Right, left, bottom, and top margins can be specified to accommodate paper size.
Borders	Allows you to specify column or row headings that will appear on each page. This option also allows you to place nonadjacent worksheet rows or columns next to one another in a printout.
Setup	Allows you to enter special control codes, such as compressed print, that are provided by the specific printer model you are using.
Other	Controls the way your data is displayed.

Additional Print Menu Commands

Command	Explanation
Line	When /PRINT PRINTER LINE is entered, 1-2-3 advances a line. This is equivalent to the line feed option on your printer.
Align	/PRINT PRINTER ALIGN tells 1-2-3 that the paper is positioned at the top of page.
Page	/PRINT PRINTER PAGE advances the paper a page. This is the equivalent to your printer's form feed or page eject option.
Clear	/PRINT PRINTER CLEAR cancels all previous printing specifications.

Activity 5-1: Printing a Spreadsheet

	Procedure	
Task	Cell Location	Enter
Retrieve EXPENSE3.		/FR EXPENSE3 [R]
Turn printer on.		
Align printer paper.		/PPA
Define the print range.		R A1..F21 [R]
Send your spreadsheet to the printer.		G
When your spreadsheet is printed, request a form feed to advance the paper.		P
Exit the Print Menu.		Q or [Esc]

Challenge

Retrieve PLAN or PERSBUDG, define a range and print the spreadsheet.

The GRAPH Command

Spreadsheets provide a tabular representation of data. Often, relationships between data can be more clearly seen if the data are viewed graphically. Lotus has the built-in capability of producing various types of graphs from data entered into a spreadsheet. If, however, you are using a computer that cannot display graphics, you will not be able to complete this unit. You might enjoy reading through it to become familiar with the Lotus procedures for graphing your spreadsheet data and refer to it when you are using a system with graphics capabilities.

Lotus 1-2-3 offers five types of graphs:

- Simple bar
- Stacked bar
- Pie charts
- Line
- XY

Graphs are created through the /GRAPH command. You may choose titles, axis labels, and legend labels in your graphs. Although you have many options available when creating graphs, there are five basic components:

- The type of graph, as listed above.
- The data range that you are graphing.
- The X range, which is the horizontal axis label in your graph.
- Graph titles.
- Legends for each data range used.

If your computer is not equipped with a graphics card, you are unable to view the graph on the screen. However, you still may create and store the graph files for printing.

When the /GRAPH command is entered, the following menu appears:

Type X A B C D E F Reset View Save Options Name Quit

The two required choices are:

■ Type   Determines the type of graph.

■ Range   (A, B, C, D, E, or F) can be either a single row or a
              column of numeric data. You must specify at least one
              range. You may specify a maximum of six data ranges per
              graph (A through F).

Sample Graphs: Pie Charts and Bar Graphs

Pie Chart

This chart uses only a single data range in your worksheet. Each
value in the range is given a "slice" of the pie. The size of the slice is
determined by a single value's portion of the total of all the values in the
data range.

Bar Graph

You can use the same data to create a bar chart. After entering
/GRAPH TYPE you specify Bar. Each number in the value range is
represented by a separate bar. 1-2-3 automatically scales the data so that
all the bars fit on the graph. Several data ranges can be displayed in a
bar chart.

Labels, Titles, and Legends

By the use of titles, labels, and legends the clarity of a graph is greatly
enhanced. On the Graph menu the next choice after the type option is
the X option. One purpose of the X option is to specify the horizontal
data range for an XY graph. Its other function is to specify a range of
labels to be placed under the horizontal axes of the Bar and Line graphs
and to label the slices of a pie chart. When the /GRAPH X command is
issued, the following appears:

Enter X-axis Range:

The worksheet range containing the labels is then supplied.

1-2-3 can place a one- or two-line title at the top of a graph. Titles can be placed on the vertical or horizontal axis. This is accomplished with the /GRAPH OPTIONS TITLES command. Titles can be a maximum of 39 characters.

Legends are used to label the data ranges. Legends are placed in graphs with the /GRAPH OPTIONS LEGEND command. You must specify the data range (A - F) and then type in a short label that describes that data range.

Naming, Saving, and Viewing Graphs

Before any graph can be printed you must store the specifications in a graph file. To save a graph, enter the command /GRAPH SAVE. You are asked to supply a filename. All of the graph settings are stored under that name. A graph filename may be the same as the worksheet filename since they are both given different extensions by 1-2-3. A graph filename is given the extension .PIC.

As mentioned previously you must have a graphics monitor in order to view a graph on the screen. To view the graph, enter the command /GRAPH VIEW. By pressing the Enter key [R], you will return to your worksheet. By pressing [F10] [Graph], you will get a picture of the most recently generated graph.

You may want to create more than one graph from the same worksheet data. With the /GRAPH NAME CREATE command you can switch from one graph to another without having to respecify your graph settings. When /GRAPH NAME CREATE is invoked, 1-2-3 stores the current graph settings under the name that you specify. To switch to a different graph enter the command /GRAPH NAME USE and the name of the graph. Please note, however, that you are not creating a separate file as in the /GRAPH SAVE command which is necessary if you want to print the graph.

/GRAPH NAME DELETE will delete an individual graph name while /GRAPH NAME RESET will delete all the graph names associated with a particular spreadsheet.

Tips for Graphing Spreadsheet Data

■ The minimum specifications for creating a graph are Type and a Data range. The exception to this is the XY graph which does require the specification of an X range.

■ You must store a graph with the /GRAPH SAVE command if you wish to print it.

■ The /GRAPH SAVE command will not save your worksheet. You must still enter the command /FILE SAVE to accomplish this.

■ X range labels should not be too long or they will overlap.

■ Legend names should not be too long.

■ If you want to save the graph names created in the /GRAPH NAME CREATE command with a particular spreadsheet, you must save the worksheet with the /FILE SAVE command after creating the the graphs.

Activity 5-2: Creating a Pie Chart

		Procedure
Task	Cell Location	Enter
Retrieve the spreadsheet EXPENSES (on the student disk).		/FR EXPENSES [R]
Create a pie chart of the data in range B11..B19.	B11	/GTPA
Anchor cell B11 with a period.		
Point to the range using the down arrow to B19 and pressing [R].	B19	[R]
Select X range to label the slices pointing to names in A11..A19 as you did above.	A11 A19	X . [R]
View the graph. Too much data is displayed to create a useful chart; notice that labels overwrite.		V
Return to the spreadsheet.		[R]
Reset the data settings.		RX[R]A[R]Q

| | Procedure | |
Task	Cell Location	Enter
Limit the data shown in the graph to the first four items.		A B11..B14[R] X A11..A14[R]
View this new graph, then return.		V [R]
Add a first title from the options menu.		OTF Average Quarterly Expenses [R]
Add a second title.		TS Salaries, Benefits Equipment, Service
Quit the Options menu and view the graph; then return.		Q V [R]
Name the graph EXPPIE using Name Create.		NC EXPPIE [R]
Save the graph as EXPPIE.		S EXPPIE [R]

Note: The pie represents the total of the four values, not the whole budget. A bar chart may be more suitable for this data.

Activity 5-3: Creating a Bar Graph

| | Procedure | |
Task	Cell Location	Enter
Create a bar graph using the same range B11..B14.		TBA [R]
Label the X axis with the same range.		X [R]
Change first title to "Quarterly Expenses."		OTF [Esc] Quarterly Expenses [R]
Quit the Options menu.		Q
View the graph.		V
Return to the spreadsheet.		[R]

	Procedure	
Task	**Cell Location**	**Enter**
Name this graph EXPBAR.		NC EXPBAR [R]
Save the Graph as EXPBAR.		S EXPBAR [R]
Exit the Graph menu.		Q
View the graph again.		[F10]
Return to the spreadsheet.		[Esc]
Save your worksheet.		/FS [R] R
You can view either named graph with the Name Use command.		/GNU EXPBAR [R] /GNU EXPPIE [R]

The PRINTGRAPH Program

Because of the size and complexity of the PRINTGRAPH program, it is not resident when you are using 1-2-3, but is instead accessed through the Lotus Access Menu after exiting the spreadsheet program. Therefore, it is important to save any graphs you create in order to be able to print them.

PRINTGRAPH is a menu-driven program allowing for output to many printers and plotters, as well as for enlargement, reduction, and rotation of graphs, and selection of different fonts for titles, legends, etc.

By selecting PRINTGRAPH from the Lotus Access Menu or simply typing PGRAPH from the prompt, you can enter the PRINTGRAPH program. A one-time configuration of the program is required and has usually been performed by the person who set up the system. Observe the data on your screen menu to see if the system is configured properly for your printer.

To print a graph or graphs, choose the IMAGE-SELECT option from the main menu. Graphs are selected by highlighting the name of the graph and pressing the SPACEBAR. Do not press [Return] until you have selected all the graphs you wish to print. Selected graphs will be marked by the pound (#) symbol.

The SETTINGS menu allows you to select color, font, size, orientation, and the interval between the printing of each selected graph. Aligning the printer by selecting ALIGN is just as important in PRINTGRAPH as it was in printing a spreadsheet. Also, as in spreadsheet printing, you must select GO for the print procedure to begin. The print procedure is quite time-consuming, thus the program has the capability to select multiple graphs for printing at one time.

Once the graph has been printed, you must return to the spreadsheet program and load the worksheet containing the graph to make changes to the graph data or labels. Remember to SAVE the corrected graph or you will still have the previous version when you return to the PRINTGRAPH program.

What Enhancements Can Be Made

There are a variety of enhancements which can be made to hard copy of 1-2-3's graphics such as:

* Increasing size

* Increasing resolution

* Changing text fonts for legends and titles

* Changing legend symbols

* Adding explanatory text

* Printing in color

* Producing presentation quality slides

Methods for Enhancing 1-2-3's Graphics

There are essentially two ways to enhance 1-2-3's graphics. They are:

Use the Lotus Print Graph Options menu to :

* change the text script.

* manually scale and rotate the graph.

* use more sophisticated printing devices
  for hardcopy.

Bring the Lotus graph into another program to:

* use the program's features to enhance the
  Lotus graph.

Using the PRINTGRAPH Menu

Once you have created and saved graphs using 1-2-3's graph menu, you can use the Lotus PRINTGRAPH utility to print them. The PRINTGRAPH disk facilitates certain enhancements to your graph depending upon the device you use to produce hard copy. The following enhancements are available on most graphics printers.

■ Eight type fonts for titles and legends

■ Manual size and rotation settings

Color is available only if you have a printing device that can produce colors. Plotters and printers capable of multiple passes will produce presentation quality hardcopy.

You will use the PRINTGRAPH menus to change fonts and size settings on the following graph.

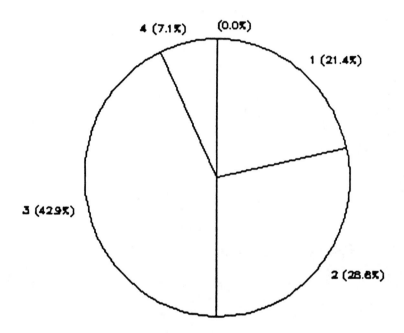

Distribution
By Race

The graph on the preceding page was produced with the print graph settings indicated by the picture of the screen that follows.

Lotus PRINTGRAPH Menu (Release 2.01)

Copyright 1986 Lotus Development Corp. All Rights Reserved. Release 2.01   MENU

Select graphs for printing
Image-Select   Settings   Go   Align   Page   Exit

GRAPH	IMAGE OPTIONS			HARDWARE SETUP
IMAGES	Size		Range Colors	Graphs Directory:
SELECTED	Top	.395	X	A:\
	Left	.750	A	Fonts Directory:
	Width	6.500	B	A:\
	Height	4.691	C	Interface:
	Rotate	.000	D	Parallel 1
			E	Printer Type:
	Font		F	
	1 BLOCK1			Paper Size
	2 BLOCK1			Width 8.500
				Length 11.000

ACTION OPTIONS
Pause: No   Eject: No

Utilizing Manual Setting Capabilities

Height and width in the following graph have been adjusted to produce a more nearly circular graph.

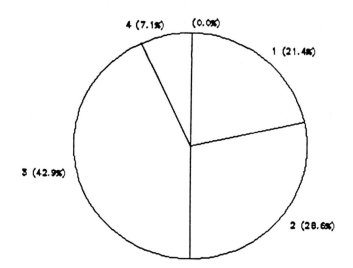

GRAPH	IMAGE OPTIONS				HARDWARE SETUP	
IMAGES	Size		Range	Colors	Graphs Directory:	
SELECTED	Top	.320	X	Black	B:\	
RACEPIE	Left	.500	A	Black	Fonts Directory:	
	Width	8.000	B	Black	A:\	
	Height	5.441	C	Black	Interface:	
	Rotate	.000	D	Black	Parallel 1	
			E	Black	Printer Type:	
	Font		F	Black	HP 2686A	
	1 BLOCK1				Paper Size	
	2 BLOCK2				Width	8.500
					Length	11.000

ACTION OPTIONS
Pause: No   Eject: No

Rotating Graphs

Selecting FULL Size (Settings, Image, Size, Full) automatically results in graph being rotated 90 degrees. Quality of fonts vary with size. Script is more presentable at FULL than at HALF size.

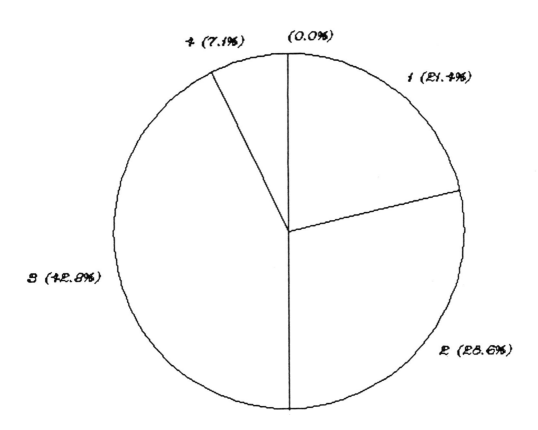

Distribution

By Row

4 (7.1%)   (0.0%)

1 (21.4%)

3 (42.8%)

2 (28.6%)

Enhancements Available through Other Programs

There are a variety of other programs available on the market that will enhance the graphics you produce from data in the 1-2-3 spreadsheet. Some of the most widely used programs include ChartMaster, Freelance, and Chart. Program capabilities vary considerably as does package price.

These programs generally accept data converted from the .WKS or .WK1 format or .PIC file generated by the 1-2-3 Graph Save command.

Once within the other program you can make one or more of the enhancements indicated at the beginning of this session.

There are many programs that advertise their capability to enhance 1-2-3 graphics. Check your local software dealer or computer magazines for the most up-to-date information.

On Your Own: Graphics Enhancements

Task

1. Select PRINTGRAPH.

2. Select the image EXPPIE.

3. Change the font to Script for both fonts.

4. Select full size.

5. Save it.

6. Print it.

Summary: Printing and Graphing Spreadsheets

- The /PRINT command gives you many options when printing a worksheet. The only required commands are:

  /PRINT PRINTER or FILE
  RANGE
  GO

- Graphs are created through the /GRAPH command. 1-2-3 offers five types of graphs: Line, Bar, XY, Stacked Bar, and Pie.

Quick Check: Printing and Graphing Spreadsheets

1. What are the required commands when printing a worksheet?

2. Name three of the five types of graphs that 1-2-3 allows.

3. What does the /GRAPH NAME CREATE command do? How is it different from the /GRAPH SAVE command?

UNIT·6·

Creating a Summary Spreadsheet

Overview: Often individual worksheets are created that contain data for a single period (month, quarter, year, etc.). It is useful to be able to combine individual worksheets into a larger summary sheet for comparison and presentation purposes. This process uses named ranges and often involves the creation and use of a template.

Skills: Understanding templates

Naming ranges

Combining files

Understanding Templates

A template is a skeleton worksheet that contains appropriate headings, labels, and formats—but no data. The template worksheet is saved as a separate file. When it is to be filled in with data, it is retrieved, completed, then saved UNDER A DIFFERENT NAME. The empty template worksheet remains on disk to be retrieved and used over and over.

A template can be created first, and data entered to conform to the template's structure. Alternately, a template can be created from a completed file by "erasing" all the data and leaving only the skeleton. A partial template for the summary spreadsheet has been created. It will be modified, enhanced, and completed.

Naming Ranges

A name can be assigned to a single cell or a cell range. These names may be up to 15 characters long. Ranges are named for the sake of clarity. For example, if you had designated a range name of "Sales" for the range A5..K5 in a worksheet, the simplest way to compute the sum would be the function @SUM(SALES).

Range names can be used in place of cell addresses in functions, formulas, and commands. Ranges must be named before you evoke a command in which you wish to use a named range. Range names are saved with the spreadsheet and will be available whenever the spreadsheet is brought into memory.

The /RANGE NAME Command has five choices:

CREATE   DELETE   LABELS   RESET   TABLE

CREATE

To name a range, use the following command:

/RANGE NAME CREATE (/RNC)

You will be prompted to enter a name and then to designate the cell or cell range to be given this name. If any cells or cell ranges have been previously named in the spreadsheet, these names will be displayed when you select the RANGE NAME CREATE command.

DELETE

Selecting DELETE enables you to delete a range name. It does not delete the range, only the current name. Referencing a deleted name will produce an error.

LABELS

A label entered into a worksheet can be used to designate the name of a neighboring cell. The /RANGE NAME LABELS command makes each label in a specified range into a name for a single cell: the cell immediately to its RIGHT, to its LEFT, above it (UP), or below it (DOWN).

RESET

RESET deletes all range names in the current worksheet. Any existing formulas or functions that used the deleted names will now refer to the cell address. Trying to use a deleted name will result in an error message.

TABLE

Use /RANGE NAME TABLE to create an alphabetical listing of all range names and their corresponding range. The range requested in this selection is the range where the program is to place the table. Be sure to place the table in an unused portion of the spreadsheet as it will over-write existing data.

Specifying Ranges

Ranges are specified by one of two methods: pointing or entering the defining (upper left and lower right) cell addresses.

In all activities requiring ranges to be specified, you will be given two choices:

1. Move the cell pointer into position before entering the Lotus command, enter the command, anchor the range at the current location with a period, and "paint" the range by moving the cursor to the specified cell address.

Example: C4.
            F6

means move to C4, enter the command, type a period to anchor the range, then move the cell pointer to F6.

2. Type in the cell addresses defining the range after entering the Lotus command.

Example: C4..F6

defines the range as C4 to F6.

Tips for Naming Ranges

■ Use a name that is meaningful, for example, SALARIES, for a column containing salary data.

■ Named ranges will retain their identity even if the entire range is later moved.

■ If you want to redefine a range that has been named, you will have to use the /RNC command to accomplish this.

■ Deleting rows or columns within a range does not require the range to be redefined and renamed.

■ If you should forget the range names that you have chosen in a specific worksheet, the [F3] [Name] function key will display a list of the range names in the current worksheet. This key can be used whenever 1-2-3 is waiting for a cell address (for example, after pressing [F5] [GOTO]). GOing TO a named range will position the pointer at the first cell of the range.

Tips for Using Named Ranges

Named ranges are particularly useful when:

■ Printing different portions of a worksheet.

■ Moving the cell pointer to different sections of a large worksheet.

■ Copying or moving a range of cells.

■ Indicating the range of cells on which a function will be performed.

■ Combining parts of various files into a larger file.

Combining Portions of Spreadsheets

It is possible to combine all or portions of several spreadsheets into one large, or summary, spreadsheet. When you RETRIEVE a file, the spreadsheet in memory is erased and the new spreadsheet takes its place. When you COMBINE files, the file in memory remains intact while all or parts of another file are read into it. The new file is read in at the current cell pointer position; therefore, it is very important to position the cell pointer before requesting a /FILE COMBINE.

FILE COMBINE requires the following steps:

- If you are combining only a part of one spreadsheet (the "outside" spreadsheet) into another, you must name the range which contains the data to be combined.

- Retrieve the file into which the outside data is to be combined.

- Position the pointer where the outside data is to appear. FILE COMBINE will overwrite data if the combine area is not blank.

- Enter the FILE COMBINE command (/FC).

- Select COPY, ADD, or SUBTRACT.

- Specify ENTIRE FILE or NAMED/SPECIFIED-RANGE.

- Specify range name (or entire file name) to combine.

- If only a range is being combined, specify the name of the file which contains that range.

- When the combination of files is complete you must examine the spreadsheet for cell references in formulas, functions and named ranged which may require correction.

- Save the combined file.

Activity 6-1: Naming Ranges

In this activity, you will be required to name data ranges in three separate databases on your student disk.

The following files are already on your student disk:

> DEPT1
> DEPT2
> DEPT3
> SUMMARY

Task	Cell Location	Procedure Enter
Load Lotus 1-2-3 into memory.		123 [R]
Give the name "DATA" to the data range in each spreadsheet beginning with DEPT1.		/FR DEPT1 [R] /RNC DATA [R]
The named data range should include only data and not the heading at the top of each column. See sample below.	A11..F15 [R]	
Save (replace) the file with its range name information.		/FS [R] R
Repeat these steps for DEPT2 and DEPT3. Note that DEPT2 has six names.		

Sample DATA Range

1	Garland	Myrtle	26-Jan-72	Clerk	14950.00
2	Wagman	Irving	27-Mar-75	Clerk	13250.00
3	O'Brien	Sarah	22-Nov-83	Supervisor	22500.00
4	Warner	Robert	30-Jun-68	Manager	38750.00
5	Johnson	Irene	14-Aug-82	Clerk	12000.00

Activity 6-2: Creating a Summary Worksheet from Named Ranges

You will combine the named data ranges to form a departmental summary database. In addition, you will be required to enter additional records to the database and format the new entries.

	Procedure	
Task	**Cell Location**	**Enter**
Retrieve the template file SUMMARY and fill in the documentation.		/FR SUMMARY[R]
Enter a Report Date using @NOW and format to DD-MMM-YY.	F7 F7	@NOW /RFD1[R]
Combine the range DATA from each spreadsheet into the file SUMMARY.	A11	/FCCN DATA[R] DEPT1[R]
Each time position the pointer on the cell in the SUMMARY file where the range should be placed before issuing the /FC command.	A16	/FCCN DATA[R] DEPT2[R]
	A22	/FCCN DATA[R] DEPT3[R]
Enter the records shown below (use @DATE for the dates). Do the rest like the following sample:	B27 C27 D27 E27 F27	Hoover[→] Hanna[→] @DATE(84,9,12)[→] Clerk[R] 11500[R]

Hoover Hanna	Sept. 12, 1984	Clerk	11500
Jones Liz	Aug. 8, 1985	Clerk	11250
White Mark	Sept. 14, 1965	Manager	42000
Gordon Jose	May 22, 1978	Supervisor	25500

Task	**Cell Location**	**Enter**
Format the hire date as DD-MMM-YY and the salary as fixed with 2 decimal places.	D27 F27	/RFD[R] D27..D30[R] /RFF[R] F27..F30[R]
Save the combined file with a new name, SUMMARY1.		/FS SUMMARY1[R]

Compare your file with the following one.

Completed Summary Worksheet

Rec. #	Lastname	First	Hire Date	Classif.	Salary	Years
1	McArthur	Alice	08-Apr-58	Clerk	11950.00	
2	Bonfield	Arturo	25-Dec-78	Supervisor	26500.00	
3	Dean	Fred	16-Jul-78	Manager	34000.00	
4	Bloom	Harry	05-Mar-80	Clerk	13500.00	
5	Levin	Zelda	31-Jan-62	Clerk	15990.00	
1	Smith	Jim	25-Mar-64	Clerk	11000.00	
2	Jones	John	02-Apr-85	Clerk	12000.00	
3	Fried	Sally	11-Dec-82	Supervisor	23000.00	
4	Wagner	Thomas	05-Aug-69	Manager	38000.00	
5	Hunter	Karen	12-Jan-85	Clerk	12125.00	
6	Smith	Sean	08-Aug-85	Clerk	11250.00	
1	Garland	Myrtle	26-Jan-72	Clerk	14950.00	
2	Wagman	Irving	27-Mar-75	Clerk	13250.00	
3	O'Brien	Sarah	22-Nov-83	Supervisor	22500.00	
4	Warner	Robert	30-Jun-68	Manager	38750.00	
5	Johnson	Irene	14-Aug-82	Clerk	12000.00	
	Hoover	Hanna	12-Sep-84	Clerk	11500.00	
	Jones	Liz	08-Aug-85	Clerk	11250.00	
	White	Mark	14-Sep-65	Manager	42000.00	
	Gordon	Jose	22-May-78	Supervisor	25500.00	

On Your Own: Summary Worksheet

Task

1. DEPT1 has made money this year, so the employees are given a salary increase as follows:

    McArthur, 15000
    Bonfield, 30000
    Dean,   35500
    Bloom,   14500
    Levin,   17500

    Make this change to the file and save it as DEPT1B.

2. File combine the new salary figures into SUMMARY1. Save it as SUM1.

UNIT·7·

Database Management

Overview: This section introduces the database management
capabilities of 1-2-3. You will use the database
summary, created in Unit VI by combining several
on-disk databases. You will modify the contents of
the combined database by adding new records and
generating a new field. You will learn how to sort,
query, and extract data from a database.

Skills: Understanding database concepts and terminology

Using DATA FILL command

Using DATE arithmetic

SORTing the database

QUERYing the database

EXTRACTing data

Lotus 1-2-3 Databases

A 1-2-3 database consists of a table of data (rows and columns) together with a row of headings for each column. The rows are called *records* and the columns are called *fields*. Each record has the same fields, although each field in every record may or may not contain an entry. The top row of field names must be included in the database.

Lotus 1-2-3 treats a database as a spreadsheet. The user directs 1-2-3 to perform database operations by using special database commands and procedures. The DATA command provides access to various database commands and procedures.

DATA commands available in 1-2-3 include:

Command	Explanation
FILL	Fills a range with consecutive values.
TABLE	Allows tables of values to be set up for input cells.
SORT	Sorts on a maximum of two key fields.
QUERY	Allows selective searches.
DISTRIBUTION	Produces a frequency distribution for a range of values.
MATRIX	Performs matrix arithmetic.
REGRESSION	Performs regression computations.
PARSE	Allows text to be broken into cell values.

DATA management terminology:

Term	Explanation
Key field(s)	Field(s) on which data is to be sorted.
Input range	Area of database to be queried; could be the entire database or a smaller range.
Criterion range	What specific data is being searched for or extracted.
Output range	Where extracted data is to be placed on the spreadsheet.

Lotus Database Components

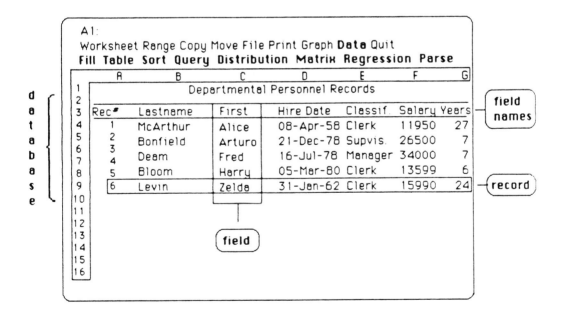

Using DATA FILL

In the following activity you will correct the record numbers into a consecutive series by using the DATA FILL command. DATA FILL allows you to specify a range of values in any increment and place that range anywhere on the spreadsheet. You will also complete the data in the Years field (column) by using a formula that includes a date function.

DATA FILL requires the following steps:

- Enter the DATA FILL command (/DF).
- Specify the range to fill.
- Specify the starting value.
- Specify the increment value.
- Specify the ending (maximum) value.

Activity 7-1: Entering a Field with Data Fill

	Procedure	
Task	Cell Location	Enter
Using SUMMARY1, enter the DATA FILL command.	A11	/DF
Specify range to fill.		A11..A30 [R]
Specify start with 1.		1 [R]
Accept increment of 1.		[R]
Accept the maximum value of 8191.		[R]

Activity 7-2: Creating a New Field (Column) Using Date Arithmetic

New fields (columns) may be added at any time to your database spreadsheet. In this activity you will generate a new field containing the number of years each employee has been with the company by subtracting hire date from today's date.

		Procedure
Task	**Cell Location**	**Enter**
Enter a formula to compute years employed by subtracting hire date from today's date and dividing by 365.	G11	(@NOW-D11) /365 [R]
Copy this formula to the other records.	G11	/C [R] G12..G30 [R]
Format these cells to have only one decimal place.	G11	/RFF1 [R] [END] [DOWN] [R]
Save your spreadsheet.		/FS [R] R

Compare your spreadsheet with the following one. Your numbers for years employed not exactly like the ones shown since the date with which hire date is compared, the date in your computer, is different. Your numbers should be greater than the example.

Database Reflecting DATA FILL and DATE Arithmetic

	A	B	C	D	E	F	G
1	Name:						
2	Div:					Created:	
3	Title:					Updated:	
4	Comments:		Summary—All Departments				
5							
6			Salary by Classification and Longevity				
7			Report Date:			\<today's date\>	
8							
9	--						
10	Rec.#	Lastname	First	Hire Date	Classif.	Salary	Years
11	1	McArthur	Alice	08-Apr-58	Clerk	11950.00	30.3
12	2	Bonfield	Arturo	25-Dec-78	Supervisor	26500.00	9.5
13	3	Dean	Fred	16-Jul-78	Manager	34000.00	10.0
14	4	Bloom	Harry	05-Mar-80	Clerk	13500.00	8.3
15	5	Levin	Zelda	31-Jan-62	Clerk	15990.00	26.5
16	6	Smith	Jim	25-Mar-64	Clerk	11000.00	24.3
17	7	Jones	John	02-Apr-85	Clerk	12000.00	3.3
18	8	Fried	Sally	11-Dec-82	Supervisor	23000.00	5.6
19	9	Wagner	Thomas	05-Aug-69	Manager	38000.00	18.9
20	10	Hunter	Karen	12-Jan-85	Clerk	12125.00	3.5
21	11	Smith	Sean	08-Aug-85	Clerk	11250.00	2.9
22	12	Garland	Myrtle	26-Jan-72	Clerk	14950.00	16.5
23	13	Wagman	Irving	27-Mar-75	Clerk	13250.00	13.3
24	14	O'Brien	Sarah	22-Nov-83	Supervisor	22500.00	4.6
25	15	Warner	Robert	30-Jun-68	Manager	38750.00	20.0
26	16	Johnson	Irene	14-Aug-82	Clerk	12000.00	5.9
27	17	Hoover	Hanna	12-Sep-84	Clerk	11500.00	3.8
28	18	Jones	Liz	08-Aug-85	Clerk	11250.00	2.9
29	19	White	Mark	14-Sep-65	Manager	42000.00	22.8
30	20	Gordon	Jose	22-May-78	Supervisor	25500.00	10.1

Sorting a Database

Having data in sorted order facilitates retrieval. Imagine trying to find a person's phone number in a telephone directory if the names were in random order!

Lotus 1-2-3's data command allows you to sort a database on a primary key—the first field or item on which the records are to be sorted—and on a secondary key for restructuring the data within the context of the primary key. In phone directories, for example, the primary key is the last name and the secondary key is the first name, so that Sam Smith comes after Bob Smith.

SORTING a database requires the following steps:

■ Enter the DATA SORT command (/DS).

■ Specify the range to be sorted.

■ Specify the primary sort key.

■ Specify the secondary sort key (optional).

Activity 7-3: Sorting a Database

In the following activity you will sort the employee database so that employees are grouped by job classification first and then by last name within a job classification. This type of sort is performed to make it easier to pull out (extract) a separate file of employees based on job classification.

Task	Procedure
Enter the data sort command.	/DS
Select Data-Range and highlight the data range to be sorted (be careful *not* to include the row containing field names).	D A11..G30 [R]
Specify the primary sort key (Classif.)—any cell in the E column can be highlighted or entered.	P E11 [R]
Select ascending sort order.	A [R]

Task	Procedure
Specify the secondary sort key (Lastname)—any cell in the B column can be highlighted or entered.	S B11 [R]
Select ascending order.	A [R]
Perform the sort.	G
Examine the data to be sure it is in sorted order by classification and last name.	
Save the spreadsheet as SUMMARY2.	/FS SUMMARY2 [R]

Sorted Database

Name:
Div: Created:
Title: Updated:
Comments: Summary—All Departments

Salary by Classification and Longevity
Report Date: <today's date>

Rec.#	Lastname	First	Hire Date	Classif.	Salary	Years
4	Bloom	Harry	05-Mar-80	Clerk	13500.00	8.3
12	Garland	Myrtle	26-Jan-72	Clerk	14950.00	16.5
17	Hoover	Hanna	12-Sep-84	Clerk	11500.00	3.8
10	Hunter	Karen	12-Jan-85	Clerk	12125.00	3.5
16	Johnson	Irene	14-Aug-82	Clerk	12000.00	5.9
18	Jones	Liz	08-Aug-85	Clerk	11250.00	2.9
7	Jones	John	02-Apr-85	Clerk	12000.00	3.3
5	Levin	Zelda	31-Jan-62	Clerk	15990.00	26.5
1	McArthur	Alice	08-Apr-58	Clerk	11950.00	30.3
11	Smith	Sean	08-Aug-85	Clerk	11250.00	2.9
6	Smith	Jim	25-Mar-64	Clerk	11000.00	24.3
13	Wagman	Irving	27-Mar-75	Clerk	13250.00	13.3
3	Dean	Fred	16-Jul-78	Manager	34000.00	10.0
9	Wagner	Thomas	05-Aug-69	Manager	38000.00	18.9
15	Warner	Robert	30-Jun-68	Manager	38750.00	20.0
19	White	Mark	14-Sep-65	Manager	42000.00	22.8
2	Bonfield	Arturo	25-Dec-78	Supervisor	26500.00	9.5
8	Fried	Sally	11-Dec-82	Supervisor	23000.00	5.6
20	Gordon	Jose	22-May-78	Supervisor	25500.00	10.1
14	O'Brien	Sarah	22-Nov-83	Supervisor	22500.00	4.6

Components of a Data Query

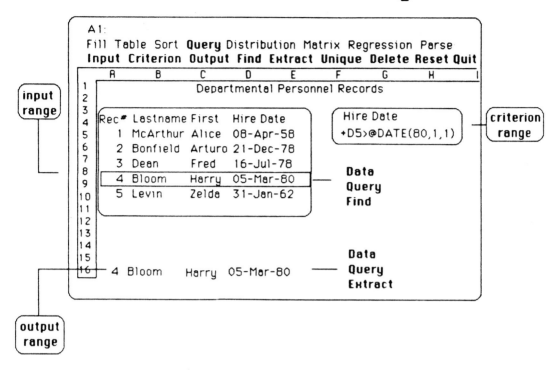

Querying the Database

The most important reason for having a database is to be able to retrieve data from it in a flexible manner. Selecting individual records or fields from a database is called querying.

Before you can do a DATA QUERY to search a 1-2-3 database, you must tell 1-2-3 which fields of the database to search, what to look for, and what part of the database to include in the search. The field(s) to search are written in row 1 of the *criterion range*. What to look for—*criterion value*—is indicated in row 2 under the appropriate field name of the *criterion range*. The part of the database to include in the search is called the *input range*. It could be the entire database.

This DATA QUERY information is set up in an empty, remote part of the spreadsheet. It is saved with the spreadsheet.

DATA QUERY requires the following steps:

- Set up a criterion range by copying field name(s) on which you wish to search to a remote part of the spreadsheet.
- Enter the criteria values immediately under the appropriate field names.
- Enter the DATA QUERY command (/DQ).
- Specify the input range.
- Specify the criterion range.
- FIND the records meeting the criteria.

Activity 7-4: Querying the Database

In the activity that follows you will query the database for all employees who have over 10 years with the company. To do so, you must first set up the criterion range with criteria (more than ten years on the job) in an unused part of the spreadsheet. Issue the DATA QUERY command, specify the INPUT range, the CRITERION range, and issue the FIND command. Records meeting the criteria are highlighted one by one; use the down arrow key to see all of them.

		Procedure	
Task	**Cell Location**	**Enter**
Using Summary2, set up a criterion range by copying field names to a blank part of the spreadsheet.	B10	/C B10..G10 [R] J10 [R]
Confirm the copy was made.		[F5] I1 [R]
Specify criteria value under the Years Field.	O11	+G11>10[R]
Return to the spreadsheet.		[F5] A10
Enter the data query command.		/DQ
Specify the input range (the entire database including field names).		I A10..G30 [R]

	Procedure	
Task	**Cell Location**	**Enter**
Specify the criterion range—field and criteria (Years and greater than 10).		C
		010..011 [R]
Find the first record meeting the criteria years >10.		F
Press the down arrow key to identify the records of the additional employees having years >10.		
Return to the command menu.		[Esc]
Quit the data command.		Q

Were all the records of those employees who have over ten years with the company found?

Tips for Querying the Database

- Field names must be put in first row of the criterion range; 32 is the limit.

- Some or all of these field names must be put in the first row of the input range and output ranges.

- No two field names may be the same.

- Do not leave any blank rows.

- Wild cards may be used in specifying criteria for finding records.

- Be sure to use a blank, remote part of the spreadsheet to write criterion, input, and output data to avoid over-writing other data.

- Save the spreadsheet to save criterion, input and output data.

- If you enter only a single row as the output range, 1-2-3 will extend the range to the bottom of the worksheet.

Data Extraction

In the previous activity you found records by simply highlighting them one at a time. In many cases users want to create a separate list (database) of records that meet some criteria.

The EXTRACT command is used to locate records meeting criteria specified in the criterion range and copy them to a separate part of the spreadsheet. EXTRACT requires all the steps used in the previous activity, with the additional step of specifying where the records are to be copied (the *output range*). Just as in specifying a criterion range, an output range must be set up before using the DATA commands and must contain the field names used in the database.

Data extraction requires the following steps:

- Set up a criterion range by copying field names you wish to search on to a remote part of the spreadsheet.

- Enter the criteria values immediately under the appropriate field name.

- Set up an output range by copying field names you wish included in the extracted database.

- Enter the DATA QUERY command (/DQ).

- Specify the input range.

- Specify the criterion range.

- Specify the output range.

- Enter the EXTRACT command (/DE).

Activity 7-5: Extracting Data from a Database

In the activity that follows you will use the same criterion range, but change the criteria used to locate records to include two conditions. You will locate all employees who are classified as clerks <u>and</u> have over twenty years' experience. You will only extract the Lastname, Years, and Salary to the output range. The first step is to set up the <u>output range</u> on an empty part of the spreadsheet.

Task	Cell Location	Procedure Enter
Establish the output range:		
Lastname	B10	/C [R] J15 [R]
Years	G10	/C [R] K15 [R]
Salary	F10	/C [R] L15 [R]
(Notice we have changed the order of the fields.)		
Add Clerk as a criterion under Classif. in the criterion range and edit Years to >20.	M11 O11	Clerk [R] +G11>20 [R]
Position screen so the criterion and output ranges are visible.		[F5] J10 [R]
Enter data query command.		/DQ
Specify input range.		I A10..G30 [R]
Specify criterion range.		C M10..O11 [R]
Specify output range.		O J15..L25 [R]
Extract data.		E
Quit the DATA command.		Q
Check to see if the extracted data meets the criteria.		
Save (replace) as SUMMARY2.		/FS [R] R

On Your Own: Databases

<u>Task</u>

All managers and supervisors are to receive training, the half with the most seniority in New York and the rest in the home office. Identify them, using the file SUMMARY2 to query and extract their records, then put them into a separate file, sort, and number.

Summary: Databases

- A 1-2-3 database is a table of rows and columns with no blank rows.
- Columns are called fields.
- Rows are called records.
- A database must have a row of field names as the first row.
- 1-2-3 stores dates as numbers representing the number of days since the turn of the century, facilitating date arithmetic.
- Modifying a database often leads to formatting changes.
- The DATA FILL command allows easy entry of a consecutive set of numbers.
- Sorting of database records can be done on two keys (primary and secondary) in ascending or descending order.
- The database may be queried for any combination of criteria that appear in the database.
- Data selected by a query can be extracted to a separate database.

Quick Check: Databases

1. What are the rows of a database called?

2. What commands would you use to place the even numbers between 0 and 40 in the range B1..B21?

3. For a mailing list database what possible keys would be useful for sorting?

4. When extracting data from a database, what are the steps taken <u>before</u> calling the DATA commands?

5. For the database used in this module, what criteria would you place in the criterion range to extract all employees making over $20,000 per year?

6. What are two advantages of range names?

Case Study #3: Databases

The Box Factory has three salespersons, Able, Baker, and Charlie. Each maintains a file of client names and addresses, together with monthly sales figures for each client.

The Factory's sales manager wants to combine all the sales figures each month into a summary showing year-to-date sales by client.

Use the file BOXFACT, and add the DATA range from the ABLE, BAKER, and CHARLIE files to get the cumulative sales figures.

UNIT·8·

Introduction to Macro Programming

Overview: An important feature of Lotus 1-2-3 is its ability to provide the user with more efficient means of creating and manipulating spreadsheet data through macro programming. In this unit you will learn the fundamentals of macro programming in addition to proper technique for their creation and execution.

Skills: Understanding macro terminology and conventions

Macro language overview

Steps in creating macros

Guidelines for writing macros

Documenting macros

Beginning a macro library

Executing and debugging macros

Macros

A macro is a two-keystroke command that will execute a set of instructions written on a spreadsheet. The process of creating a macro is called macro programming.

The types of operations that macros are used to perform include:

Automating Commands	-	Naming Ranges Printing Saving Files Widening Columns
Getting User Input	-	Data entry Decision making
System Control	-	Controlling the flow of operations through automated procedures and menus

In general, any data entry or 1-2-3 commands that you perform interactively can be written into a set of instructions for later execution as a macro.

Whenever you have spreadsheet procedures that must be done often or repetitiously, you can enhance your speed, efficiency and accuracy by using macros to reduce the number of steps you have to perform manually.

Basic Macro Language

1-2-3 uses an abbreviated language in its macros. For the most part, the vocabulary can be broken down into categories by the task a macro is to perform.

■ Sequences of text or command keys.

> Sales Summary
> /WGFF1

■ Pointer or cursor movement keys.

> {UP},{DOWN},{LEFT}
> {RIGHT},{HOME},{GOTO}
> {PGUP},{PGDN},{END}
> {TAB},{WINDOW}

■ Function and editing keys.

> {DEL},{EDIT},{ABS}
> {TABLE},{NAME},{GRAPH}
> {ESC},{BS},{QUERY},{CALC}

■ Getting keyboard input.

{?}	Store response at current location.
{GETLABEL prompt, location}	Pause, display message, store response as label in location.
{GETNUMBER prompt, location}	Pause, display message, store response as value in location.

■ Controlling program sequence.

{If condition} action alternate action	If condition is true, then perform action. If condition is false, then perform alternate action.
{BRANCH location}	Continue at location.
{routine name}	Call a subroutine.
{RETURN}	Return from a subroutine.
{QUIT}	Quit macro to Ready mode.
{MENUBRANCH location}	Run a menu.

Steps in Creating and Using a Macro

Generally the creation and use of macros to execute command sequences follows these steps:

Steps

- *Perform* the operation manually; *write* on paper the keystrokes required.

- *Translate* keystrokes to macro language where necessary, for example, replace all [Returns] with ~ (tildes).

- *Enter* (type) the sequence in macro work area.

- *Name* the macro.

  A special range name convention is used in naming macros. The macro (only the first cell must be named) is named as a backslash \ followed by a single letter, for example, \S.

- *Run* the macro by typing [Alt] and the letter in the macro name.

Guidelines for Writing Macros

- A part of the worksheet, generally diagonally positioned from the data section, should be set aside for macros. This arrangement allows rows and columns to be inserted into the spreadsheet without altering the layout of the macros.

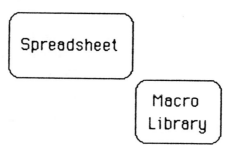

■ Any macro that does not begin with a label must be preceded by the label prefix, ', for example, enter the FILE SAVE command as '/FS.

■ Use the following representations:

~ (tilde) indicates the [Return] key

{ } (braces) surround names of keys and advanced built-in Lotus macro procedures

{?} stops the sequence of commands to allow for user input

■ Macros may extend horizontally across the worksheet, or for clarity, may be typed in sections in a contiguous column. Note that the first macro is in cell A1; the second in D1..D3.

	A	B	C	D
1	This is a correct macro layout.			This is also
2				a correct macro
3				layout.
4				

■ All macros terminate with a blank row.

Documenting Macros

As you begin to accumulate macros on your spreadsheet, it will be useful to have some area that identifies the text of the macro with its name and use.

While how a macro is documented is up to the writer, there are some conventions which are recommended.

Macro Documenting Conventions

Place macros in a single area of the worksheet

Place the name consistently to the left, right, or above the macro

Place the description of its use consistently to the left, right, or above the macro.

Name the range in which macros reside "Macro Library" or something similar.

Creating and Documenting a Macro Library

A macro library is a collection of macros in one location on your spreadsheet. Macro libraries generally include the macro label, the macro definition, and a comment describing what the macro does for future reference. There are many ways to lay out a macro library. You will learn one way in this course; later you may develop a different method on your own.

Since the approximate size of the spreadsheet model for this course is known, it is easy to choose a location for the macro library. When developing your own spreadsheets, choose a location that is diagonal to the bottom, right cell of the spreadsheet. As the spreadsheet expands, the macro library will move with it.

Activity 8-1: Setting Up a Macro Library

Task	Cell Location	Procedure Enter
Turn on your computer and load DOS if it is not on your Lotus system disk.		
Load Lotus 1-2-3 into memory.		123
Retrieve SUMMARY.		/FR SUMMARY [R]
Position the cell pointer.	M55	
Enter the labels shown below:		

```
          M      N       O      P     Q     R      S
54
55  MACRO LIBRARY
56  ================================================================
57  LABEL      MACRO                                      COMMENTS
58
```

Task	Cell Location	Procedure Enter
Name the macro range.	M55	/RNC MACROS [R] [R]
Save the worksheet as SUMMAC.		/FS SUMMAC [R]

Executing and Debugging Macros

After a macro has been designed, written on the spreadsheet in an appropriate place, labeled, and named, it is time to be tested. Employ the following techniques to test and debug your macros.

- Save your spreadsheet each time before testing a macro. A faulty macro can overwrite data or hang up your computer causing you to reboot and lose data that has not been saved.

- Position the cell pointer before invoking a macro that is to act on a specific group of cells.

- Type [Alt] and the macro label, for example, [P], to begin macro execution.

- Press [Ctrl][Break] followed by [Esc] to interrupt an executing macro.

- Invoke the STEP mode, [Alt][F2], to watch the macro proceed one step at a time making debugging an easier task.

On Your Own: Macro Wish List

Task

Make a "wish list" of some of the operations in Lotus that you would like to automate.

UNIT·9·

Writing and Executing Macros

Overview: Macros provide an effective tool for automating and managing worksheets. In this unit, you will design, write, document, test, and debug macros ranging from the simple to the complex.

Skills: Text entry macros

Cursor control macros

Command macros

Macros requiring user input

Macros incorporating built-in commands

Activity 9-1: Creating a Text Macro

Documentation is an important aspect of all spreadsheet creation. Since this is a repetitive task, it is ideal for a macro. In this activity you will write your first macro that will enter your name and division into the worksheet at the cursor position.

Task	Procedure Cell Location	Enter
Using SUMMAC, note the documentation area in B1..B2.		[HOME]
GOTO the special macro section called MACROS.		[F5] MACROS [R]
Enter your first macro in the column entitled "MACRO."	N59	<your name>~ [R]
Name the macro \T (for Title).	M59	'\T [R]
Use the /RANGE NAME LABELS RIGHT command to name the macro in N59 that will print your name.	M59	/RNLR [R]
Document the macro.	S59	Enter name [R]
GOTO B1 and test the macro.	B1	[Alt] [T]
Add a second line that gives your division initials.	N60	<your division>~[R]
You do not need to rename the macro since macros continue to execute down a column until a blank line is reached.		
Test the macro.	B1	[Alt] [T]
Add the instructions to move the cursor to the next row.	N59	<your name> {DOWN} [R]
Test the macro again.	B1	[Alt] [T]
Edit the documentation.	S59	Enter name and division [R]
Save the worksheet before going to each new activity.		/FS [R] R

Activity 9-2: Creating Command Macros

Any command sequence that can be entered into Lotus can be trans-
lated into a macro. The following steps are required when creating a
command macro.

■ *Perform* the operation manually; *write* on paper the keystrokes
required.

■ *Translate* keystrokes to macro language where necessary, for example,
replace [R] (return) with ~ (tilde); put ' (label prefix) before a
command (/).

■ *Enter* (type) the sequence.

■ *Name* the macro.

■ *Execute* the macro by typing [Alt] and the letter of the macro name.

		Procedure
Task	**Cell Location**	**Enter**
Write the procedure to resave a file under the same name.		/FS [R] R
Convert to macro language.		'/FS~R
GOTO the macro library.		[F5] MACROS [R]
Enter macro as a label.	N62	'/FS~R [R]
Enter the macro name as a label.	M62	'\S [R]
Name the macro.	M62	/RNLR [R]
Document the macro.	S62	File save with Replace [R]
Execute the macro.		[Alt] [S]

Note: The macro symbol {?} halts the sequence of commands until the
user inputs a response and presses [R]. In general practice you
might want to include this symbol in your File Save macro to
prevent overwriting a file. For this course you will use the
simple File Save Replace macro.

Lotus 1-2-3

Activity 9-3: Creating a Macro to Name a Range

A command sequence you will use throughout this course is the /RANGE NAME LABELS RIGHT command to name your macros. Macros must be named before they can be used. It would be handy to have a macro enter this command sequence for you, naming the macro to the right of each label.

Task	Cell Location	Procedure Enter
Write the command for /RANGE NAME LABELS RIGHT.		/RNLR [R]
Enter the macro into N64, enter the name \N into M64, and name it using /RNLR.	N64 M64 M64	'/RNLR~[R] '\N [R] /RNLR [R]
Document the macro.	S64	Range Name Labels Right [R]
Save the spreadsheet containing these macros.		[ALT] [S]

Use this macro to name the macros you create in the following activities.

Activity 9-4: Creating a Macro to Automate File Combination

FILE COMBINE is a powerful Lotus capability. It allows merging of several files into one without destroying the integrity of the main spreadsheet. In this activity, you will combine named ranges of data from several departments into the base spreadsheet SUMMAC.

		Procedure	
Task	**Cell Location**	**Enter**	
On paper, write the procedure to FILE COMBINE into SUMMAC at A11 the named range DATA from DEPT1.	A11	/FCCN DATA [R] DEPT1 [R]	
Translate the keystrokes into macro language, where necessary.		'/FCCN DATA~ DEPT1~	
Go to the macro library.		[F5] MACROS	
Enter the macro sequence as a label, with the filename, DEPT1, on the next line.	N66 N67	'/FCCNDATA~ [R] DEPT1~[R]	
Place the macro name to its left.	M66	'\C[R]	
Use the macro you just made to name this macro.	M66	[Alt] [N]	
Document the macro.	S66	Combine named ranges [R]	
To execute the macro, position the pointer where the data is to appear and execute the macro.	A11	[Alt] [C]	
Save the SUMMAC file containing the combine macro and DEPT1 data.		[ALT] [S]	

Activity 9-5: A Macro to Combine Files with User Input

To FILE COMBINE more departments into the SUMMAC worksheet, you could write a new macro for each department. Or, you could design a macro that could be used for *any* department that the user designates at the time the macro is executed.

		Procedure
Task	Cell Location	Enter
Edit the macro \C.	N66	[F2]
Replace the named range and file with a {?} which allows the user to input the desired range and file.	N67	'/FCCN{?}~ [R] {?}~[R]
Position the pointer and execute the macro.	A16	[Alt] [C]
Respond to request for user input of range name.		DATA [R]
Respond to request for user input of file name.		DEPT2 [R]
Examine the combined file. If it is correct, invoke the macro again and bring in the DATA range from the file DEPT3 as you did for DEPT2.	A22	[Alt] [C]
Use the DATA FILL command to renumber the Rec. # field.	A11	/DF A11..A26 [R] 1 [R] 1 [R] [R]
Save the file.		[Alt] [S]

Activity 9-6: A Macro to Facilitate Date Entry

The @DATE(yy,mm,dd) function can be very tedious to enter repeatedly. Macros can ease the job of entering the date or any other Lotus function into spreadsheets.

		Procedure
Task	Cell Location	Enter
Write the steps for the @DATE function.		@DATE(yy,mm,dd) [R]
Translate it into Lotus macro language accepting user input for yy, mm, and dd.		'@DATE({?}, {?},{?})~
GOTO the macro section.	[F5]	MACROS [R]
Enter this macro into N69.	N69	'@DATE({?}, {?},{?})~[R]
Place the name \D in M69.	M69	'\D[R]
Use the range name macro to name this macro.	M69	[ALT] [N]
Document the macro.	S69	Enter date function [R]
Save the spreadsheet, before you test a new macro!		[Alt] [S]
Use the macro to revise the dates in cells D22 through D26 as below.	D22	[ALT] [D] 78 [R] 2 [R] 25 [R]
Save the file.		[ALT] [S]

D

22 February 25, 1978
23 May 12, 1983
24 June 29, 1969
25 February 13, 1981
26 December 20, 1982

Activity 9-7: A Macro to Format Dates

Since Lotus enters all dates in serial (or Julian) format, they must always be formatted to be "human-readable." You will design a macro to format a column to dates D1 format.

Task	Cell Location	Procedure Enter
Manually perform (up to the last carriage return) and write on paper the procedure to format a column of dates.		/RFD1. [END] [DOWN]
Translate.		'/RFD1.{END} {DOWN}~
GOTO the macro section.		[F5] MACROS [R]
Enter the macro.	N71	'/RFD1.{END} {DOWN}~[R]
Name the macro \Y for year.	M71 M71	'\Y [R] [Alt] [N]
Document the macro.	S71	Format date column [R]
Save the file.		[ALT] [S]
Test the macro.	D22	[Alt] [Y]

Activity 9-8: A Macro to Format Columns to Fixed Format

Spreadsheet data invariably needs to be formatted. This is an excellent time to develop a macro that will format a continuous column of data to FIXED format allowing the user to input the number of decimal places.

Task	Cell Location	Procedure Enter
Write the steps to format a column of data to fixed format. Remember the [END] [DOWN] sequence will define a range to the end of a continuous column.		/RFF<0,1,2> [R] [END] [DOWN] [R]
Translate.		'/RFF{?}~ {END} {DOWN}~
GOTO the macro section and enter.	N73	'/RFF{?}~ {END} {DOWN}~ [R]
Name the macro \F for format.	M73	'\F [R] [Alt] [N]
Document the macro.	S73	Format fixed column [R]
Save the file.		[Alt] [S]
Before testing this macro, enter the formula to calculate years employed.	G11	(@NOW-D11) /365 [R]
Copy to G12..G26.	G11	/C [R] G12..G26 [R]
Now test the macro by formatting column G to 1 decimal place.	G11	[Alt] [F] 1 [R]

Spreadsheet Reflecting New Formats

	A	B	C	D	E	F	G
9	---						
10	Rec.#	Lastname	First	Hire Date	Classif.	Salary	Years
11	1	McArthur	Alice	08-Apr-58	Clerk	11950.00	30.3
12	2	Bonfield	Arturo	25-Dec-78	Supervisor	26500.00	9.5
13	3	Dean	Fred	16-Jul-78	Manager	34000.00	10.0
14	4	Bloom	Harry	05-Mar-80	Clerk	13500.00	8.3
15	5	Levin	Zelda	31-Jan-62	Clerk	15990.00	26.5
16	6	Smith	Jim	25-Mar-64	Clerk	11000.00	24.3
17	7	Jones	John	02-Apr-85	Clerk	12000.00	3.3
18	8	Fried	Sally	11-Dec-82	Supervisor	23000.00	5.6
19	9	Wagner	Thomas	05-Aug-69	Manager	38000.00	18.9
20	10	Hunter	Karen	12-Jan-85	Clerk	12125.00	3.5
21	11	Smith	Sean	08-Aug-85	Clerk	11250.00	2.9
22	12	Garland	Myrtle	26-Jan-72	Clerk	14950.00	16.5
23	13	Wagman	Irving	27-Mar-75	Clerk	13250.00	13.3
24	14	O'Brien	Sarah	22-Nov-83	Supervisor	22500.00	4.6
25	15	Warner	Robert	30-Jun-68	Manager	38750.00	20.0
26	16	Johnson	Irene	14-Aug-82	Clerk	12000.00	5.9

Activity 9-9: Creating a Print Macro

'To print a Lotus spreadsheet requires a minimum of *seven* keystrokes, /PRINT PRINTER RANGE [Return] ALIGN GO QUIT, and can double if any print options are selected. A macro is certainly appropriate here. You will design a basic print macro, and then, if time allows, incorporate advanced features to allow for print options to be included.

		Procedure
Task	**Cell Location**	**Enter**
Write the basic procedure to print a spreadsheet.		/PPR <range> [R] [A] [G] [Q]
Translate to macro language.		'/PPR {?}.{?}~ AGQ
Enter this macro.	N75	'/PPR {?}.{?}~ AGQ [R]
Name the macro.	M75	'\P [R] [Alt] [N]
Document the macro.	S75	Print user-defined range [R]
Save before testing.		[ALT] [S]
Turn on your printer, adjust paper, and test the print macro.		[Alt] [P]

Completed Macro Library

	M	N	O	----	R	S	T
55	MACRO LIBRARY						
56	==						
57	LABEL	MACRO			COMMENTS		
58							
59	\T	JANE DOE {DOWN}			Enter name and division		
60		OED-IRM~					
61							
62	\S	/FS~R			File save with replace		
63							
64	\N	/RNLR~			Range Name Labels Right		
65							
66	\C	/FCCN{?}~			Combine named ranges		
67		{?}~					
68							
69	\D	@DATE({?},{?},{?})~			Enter date function		
70							
71	\Y	/RFD1.{END}{DOWN}~			Format date column		
72							
73	\F	/RFF{?}~{END}{DOWN}			Format fixed column		
74							
75	\P	/PPR{?}.{?}~AGQ			Print user-defined range		
76							

On Your Own: Writing and Executing Macros

Task

1. Using the "wish list" you made in the On Your Own exercise in Unit VIII, write a few macros, adding them to MACLIB. Refer to Unit VIII, particularly Basic Macro Language and Steps in Creating and Using a Macro.

2. Choose an additional print option, for example, in setting up for compressed printing, and incorporate it into your macro.

UNIT ·10·

Advanced Macro Concepts and Applications

Overview: Macros can be used to create customized "user friendly" applications in 1-2-3. Combined into menus, extracted into libraries, and integrated into automatically loading spreadsheets, macros can always be accessible to enhance the use of Lotus 1-2-3.

Skills: Designing and creating macro menus

Using advanced macro keywords to control program flow

Extracting a portion of a spreadsheet

Creating an automatically loading macro

Creating Macro Menus

The macros you have created facilitate the automation of individual spreadsheet *tasks*. Taking this capability one step further, macros can be combined in such a way as to create an automated *system*. One way of doing this is through the creation of custom menus which operate like 1-2-3's command menus.

The steps for creating a menu are:

- Design the content of the menu, using a special layout on the spreadsheet.

- Name the menu as a regular range.

- Create a macro using a special macro command {MENUBRANCH menuname} to execute the menu.

- Name the {MENUBRANCH menuname} macro as a macro range, using a backslash-single letter combination.

- Run the menu by executing the {MENUBRANCH menuname} macro with [Alt]-single letter, as you would any other macro.

You will explore each of these steps as you design a menu system to execute the macros you have created.

Designing the Menu

The creation of a menu requires a special layout on the spreadsheet. The general form of the layout appears below:

Menu Design

Option 1	Option 2	Option 3	Option 8
Description	Description	Description	Description
Step 1	Step 1	Step 1	Step 1
Step 2	Step 2	Step 2	Step 2
. . . .	. . . .	. . . .	. . . .
Final Step	Final Step	Final Step	Final Step
Blank row ·	Blank row	Blank row	Blank row

Where:

- OPTIONS are written in contiguous columns across a row. A blank column ends the option list. Upon execution of the menu macro, the options appear in the command area just as 1-2-3 command menu choices do. They operate in the same manner—they can be selected by pointing or by typing their first letter.

- The DESCRIPTION written on the row just below each option will appear below the menu when the corresponding option is highlighted.

- The STEPS written below an option are executed upon selection of that option from the menu.

Your menu will have six options (up to eight options are allowed):

Combine   Format   Print   Save   Ready   Quit

When this menu is executed, it will appear in the 1-2-3 control panel just as any other menu does. The user can choose, by typing the first letter of the option or by highlighting the option and pressing [RETURN], any of the menu options.

- Combine prenamed ranges into a summary spreadsheet.

- Format a range using either a date format or a user-defined fixed format.

- Print a user-defined range and quit print menu.

- Save the current worksheet.

- Return to READY mode to allow movement around the spreadsheet.

- Exit 1-2-3 while automatically updating the documentation section of the worksheet and saving the file.

The second line of the menu contains the descriptions of the highlighted command. These are entered in the row directly below the corresponding option.

Activity 10-1: Designing a Menu—Option and Description Lines

The menu will be constructed in the macro section of the worksheet, columns N through S. To make the menu easier to read while it is being constructed, it would be useful to widen those columns to 20 spaces.

		Procedure
Task	**Cell Location**	**Enter**
Widen the columns used for the menu.	N79	/WCS20 [R]
Repeat the above procedure in O79, P79, Q79, and R79.		
Enter options.	N79	Combine
	O79	Format
	P79	Print
	Q79	Save
	R79	Ready
	S79	Quit
Enter descriptions.	N80	Combine named ranges
	O80	Date or fixed format
	P80	Print user-defined range
	Q80	Save the file
	R80	Return to READY
	S80	Update, save, return to DOS
Name the menu.	M79	MENU [R] [Alt] [N]

Entering Macros into the Menu

The third line (and as many additional lines as necessary) contains the macro (steps to be performed) that will execute when the corresponding option is chosen. You will develop each of the options separately, then you will enter the macros as part of the menu. The completed menu is shown following Activity 10-3.

Menu Option: Combine (Subroutine Branch)

The required steps to combine files with user input are identical to the ones that make up your \C macro:

/FCCN{?}~{?}~

You could retype this sequence as the third menu line under the Combine option. When the Combine option is chosen, the File Combine macro will be executed.

However, an easier alternative is to refer back to the already-created macro. You can accomplish this with the advance macro facility {subroutine}. Enclosing the macro name, \C ,in braces {\C} tells 1-2-3 to branch to the named location, execute the commands it finds there, and then return to the original routine—the menu.

The third line of the Combine option, therefore, is:

{\C}

When the Combine procedure (the subroutine) is completed, control will return to the next line of the menu macro. If nothing is there, the macro will end.

It would be useful to have the menu reappear for further choices. You can recall the menu with the {MENUBRANCH} macro naming the location to branch to, MENU.

{MENUBRANCH MENU}

Menu Option: Format (Menucall Branch)

The second menu option actually produces two further options, Date Format or Fixed Format. There must be a way for the user to choose between these options and then execute the appropriate commands. One way to make choices is from another menu. We can instruct the original menu to temporarily pass control to another menu, process the choices from that menu, then return for further choices from the original menu. The macro keyword that will accomplish this is:

{MENUCALL menuname}

In the following activity, you will create a submenu and name it FMTMENU; therefore, the third line of the Format option will be:

{MENUCALL FMTMENU}

The fourth line restarts the main menu:

{MENUBRANCH MENU}

* * * * * * *

	N	O
79	Combine	Format
80	Combine named ranges	Date or fixed format
81	{\C}	{MENUCALL FMTMENU}
82	{MENUBRANCH MENU}	{MENUBRANCH MENU}

Activity 10-2: Creating the Format Submenu

	Procedure	
Task	**Cell Location**	**Enter**
Construct the format submenu.		
Enter the option names.	N85	Fixed
	O85	Date
Enter the descriptions.	N86	Fixed format
	O86	Date format #1
Refer back to the format macros.	N87	{\F}
	O87	{\Y}
Instruct the program to RETURN to the main menu immediately following the MENUCALL.	N88	{RETURN}
	O88	{RETURN}
Name this menu macro.	M85	FMTMENU [R] [Alt] [N]

* * * * * * *

	N	O
85	FMTMENU Fixed	Date
86	Fixed format	Date format #1
87	{\F}	{\Y}
88	{RETURN}	{RETURN}

Menu Option: Print

This option is like the Combine and Save options: the appropriate
already-created macro is called as a subroutine and then the menu is
displayed again. The subroutine is \P, the Print macro. When the
subroutine is complete, control will return to the main menu. The
command {MENUBRANCH MENU} restarts the main menu.

The third line is:

{\P}

The fourth line is:

{MENUBRANCH MENU}

* * * * * *

P

79	Fixed
80	Print user-defined range
81	{\P}
82	{MENUBRANCH MENU}

Menu Option: Save

This option is like the Combine option: the appropriate already-created macro is called as a subroutine and then the menu is displayed
again. The subroutine is \S, the File Save macro. When the subroutine
is complete, control will return to the main menu. The command
{MENUBRANCH MENU} restarts the main menu.

The third line is:

{\S}

The fourth line is:

{MENUBRANCH MENU}

* * * * * * *

Q

79   Save
80   Save the file
81   {\S}
82   {MENUBRANCH MENU}

Menu Option: Ready (Exit from Macro)

There will be tasks that are not contained in the menu (movement around the spreadsheet, copying, entering data) which the user will need to perform during the creation of any spreadsheet. There must be a way for the user to exit the menu while still retaining the current spreadsheet. Every menu must contain a choice which allows the menu to stop.

EXIT is often the option used for this purpose. In our menu, how- ever, EXIT could be confused with the QUIT option. Therefore, we'll call our exiting option READY (return to Ready mode).

The macro keyword {QUIT} does just that—allows the user to quit from the macro. Pressing any key following the execution of this option returns 1-2-3 to Ready mode.

The third line of the READY option is

{QUIT}

* * * * * * *

R

79   Ready
80   Return to Ready
81   {QUIT}

Menu Option: Quit

This last menu option allows the user to safely leave the SUMMAC spreadsheet. QUITting through the menu prevents the user from forgetting to save the final version of the spreadsheet. The Quit menu can also automate documentation, showing the last time the spreadsheet was used.

The steps which this menu option will execute are:

- Provide the current date so that the next time time this file is retrieved, the "Updated" cell will accurately reflect the last time the spreadsheet was used.

- Save the file after the "Updated" date is entered. Even if the file was recently saved, this prevents quitting without saving the absolute final version.

- Quit 1-2-3 and return to the DOS prompt.

* * * * *

The first step will be to write the macro for the current date to be placed in G3. The macro {LET location,string} instructs 1-2-3 to enter a predetermined string (values or labels) at the location specified. The @NOW function returns the current date. This function will produce the value we want to appear in the Updated cell, G3:

{LET G3,@NOW}

It would be useful to be at the HOME position when the worksheet is finally saved. The replacement of the Updated information can then be seen by the user, and the next time the file is retrieved, it will appear with the cell pointer at the HOME position. (A file is retrieved with the cell pointer in the same position it was when the file was last saved.)

The next step in the Quit option will be to position the pointer at cell A1:

{HOME}

Cell G3 was previously formatted with the date #1 format, so when the @NOW function is entered, it will type the date as specified.

With the Updated cell now reflecting the current date, we can save the file. When it is later retrieved, the Updated cell will indicate that "today" was when this worksheet was last used.

The already-created \S macro can be entered as a subroutine call to accomplish this:

{\S}

Finally, we want to exit 1-2-3 and return to the DOS prompt. We have no macro which will do this. We can enter that command as the final step in the Quit option.

The manual steps in quitting 1-2-3 are / (to invoke the command menu), Q (to choose Quit), and Y (to confirm YES). Those exact steps can be entered here.

'/QY

* * * * * * *

	S	T	U
79	Quit		
80	Update,save,return to DOS		
81	{LET G3, @NOW}		
82	{HOME}		
83	{\S}		
84	/QY		

Activity 10-3: A "Run Menu" Macro

After the menu is designed and named, a macro must be created (and named) whose purpose is to "call" or initiate the execution of the menu.

Task	Cell Location	Procedure Enter
Create the special macro which will run the MENU menu.	N90	{MENUBRANCH MENU}
Name this macro.	M90	'\M [R] [Alt] [N]
Executing this macro [Alt] [M] will run the completed menu.		
Execute the menu, save the file, and return to READY mode.		[Alt] [M] S [R] RR
Experiment with the menu. Manually reformat the date ranges to a general format.	D11	/RFG [End] [Down] [R]
Call the menu, and format that range as Date Format #1	D11	[Alt] [M] F D R

Completed Macro Menu

^A

	M	N	O	P
78				
79	MENU	Combine	Format	Print
80		Combine named ranges	Date or fixed format	Print user-defined
81		{\C}	{MENUCALL FMTMENU}	{\P}
82		{MENUBRANCH MENU}	{MENUBRANCH MENU}	{MENUBRANCH MENU}
83				
84				
85	FMTMENU	Fixed	Date	
86		Fixed format	Date format #1	
87		{\F}	{\Y}	
88		{RETURN}	{RETURN}	
89				
90	\M	{MENUBRANCH MENU}		

- - - - - - - - - - - - - - - - - - -

	Q	R	S	T	U
78					
79	Save	Ready	Quit		
80	Save the file	Return to Ready	Update,save,return to DOS		
81	{\S}	{QUIT}	{LET G3, @NOW}		
82	{MENUBRANCH MENU}		{HOME}		
83			{\S}		
84			/QY		
85					
86					

Extracting a Portion of a Spreadsheet

Just as individual worksheets can be COMBINED into a larger summary worksheet, parts of large spreadsheets can be EXTRACTED to form individual files. For presentation purposes, to limit the amount of data accessible for viewing, or to generate additional files from which other composite spreadsheets can be created, it is often necessary to save a portion of a worksheet separately.

Extracting a portion of a worksheet does not alter that portion in any way. A copy of the extracted area becomes a new file. The worksheet from which the copy is made is not changed. Contrary to the usual definition of the word, EXTRACT does not REMOVE a portion of the spreadsheet.

The macro section of SUMMAC could be extracted as a complete and separate macro library. Macros function only within the worksheet where they were created and named as ranges. To use your macros or menus in any other worksheet, you would have to create and name them again. Alternately, you could have all your macros stored in a separate file, MACLIB. That file could be COMBINED with any other spreadsheet, and with a few adjustments (named ranges, for example, are not transferred during a File Combine procedure) those macros would be usable in any other worksheet.

Activity 10-4: Extracting the Macro Library

Task	Cell Location	Procedure Enter
Begin the FILE EXTRACT procedure to create a separate file containing all the macros.	M55	/FX
Choose Values (no formulas are involved).		V
Name the new file.		MACLIB [R]
Enter the range to be extracted.		M55..S90 [R]
View your new macro library.		/FR MACLIB [R]
Confirm that all the range names have also been extracted, and relate to the proper macro.		[F5] [F3]

Creating a Worksheet Template Containing the Macro Library

It would be convenient to have these macros available for use whenever you begin a new spreadsheet. Just as you began your SUMMARY spreadsheet from a predesigned and formatted template, any worksheet can begin with an already-created template.

You can COMBINE the file MACLIB into an appropriate area of an empty spreadsheet, and save it as MACTEMP. Anytime you want to start a new spreadsheet, you can retrieve MACTEMP, enter your data and use the macros, and then save it under a different name. The macros are always available without having to be recreated. More macros can always be added, or existing macros can be edited to make them more useful in individual worksheets.

There are some very important differences between this File Combine procedure and a File Retrieve procedure.

- When MACLIB was *Retrieved* in the Activity 10-4, it retained its named ranges.

- When MACLIB was *Retrieved* in the Activity 10-4, the worksheet currently on the screen (SUMMAC) was "erased."

- When MACLIB was *Retrieved*, the upper left cell appeared as A1, regardless of where your cell pointer was when you issued the /FR command.

* * * * *

- When a file is *Combined*, it loses any range names it might have had when it was extracted. (This is a problem with a macro library since unnamed macros cannot be used.)

- When a file is *Combined*, it does not "push out" the worksheet that is currently open; it becomes a part of it.

- When a file is *Combined*, it enters the current worksheet at the cell pointer position.

- When a file is *Combined*, it enters the current worksheet using the column widths and formats of the worksheet into which it is being combined.

Activity 10-5: Creating a Template Containing the Macro Library

Task	Cell Location	Procedure Enter
Erase the current worksheet.		/WEY
On this new worksheet, go to an appropriate area for the macro library.		[F5] AA100 [R]
File Combine MACLIB into this empty worksheet.	AA100	/FCCE MACLIB [R]
Examine the newly combined spreadsheet. Try to GOTO a macro by using its name. Look at the menu macro.		
Use RANGE NAME LABELS RIGHT to rename the macros.		/RNLR AA104..AA135 [R]
Name the cell in AA100 MACROS.	AA100	/RNC MACROS [R] [R]
Try to GOTO a particular macro.		[F5] \Y [R]
Return to cell A1, then go quickly to the macro section.		[F5] MACROS [R]
Expand the menu columns so the labels are readable.	AB123 AC123 AD123 AE123 AF123	/WCS20 [R] /WCS20 [R] /WCS20 [R] /WCS20 [R] /WCS20 [R]
Save this template as MACTEMP.		/FS MACTEMP [R]

Automatic Loading of Worksheets

When 1-2-3 begins execution, it automatically searches the current disk directory for a worksheet named AUTO123. If such a file exists, 1-2-3 automatically File Retrieves it. The "current disk directory" when 1-2-3 starts execution is determined by the setting in the 1-2-3 configuration file. This can be changed with the /Worksheet Global Default Directory command.

Any worksheet can be named AUTO123. If you usually begin a new spreadsheet when starting 1-2-3, you might want to rename MACTEMP to become the automatic-loading AUTO123. This would give you a blank work area with the macro library available each time you start the program.

If most of your 1-2-3 work involves manipulating or adding to an existing spreadsheet, it might be convenient to name that spreadsheet AUTO123 and eliminate having to /FR the same file at every work session.

Very often, an AUTO123 file contains the opening screen and/or main menu of a fully automated system from which a user will make menu choices.

If an AUTO123 file is no longer needed, or if it would be more convenient to have a different one, it can be "unautomated" by being renamed.

On Your Own: Autoload Macro

Task

Make your macro library autoloading.

UNIT ·11·

Auto-executing Macros

Overview: This section explores the special auto-executing macro, as well as additional advanced macro keywords and concepts.

Skills: Understanding and creating a \0 macro

Using macros to make decisions

Automatically Executing Macros

Macros must be called by the [Alt]-single letter combination of keystrokes. This means that there can be only 26 macros (A through Z) on any spreadsheet which can be individually called by the [Alt]-letter combination. (Other macros, of course, can be created with other names—such as the MENU and FMTMENU macros—which can be combined with and called from the backslash + single-letter macros.)

You can assign one additional macro name: \0 (zero). This is a special name, indicating an auto-execute macro.

If a worksheet that you have created includes a macro named \0, 1-2-3 automatically starts the macro whenever you load that worksheet. This feature may be particularly useful in combination with an AUTO123 autoloading worksheet.

We will create a \0 macro on the SUMMAC worksheet which will automatically fill in appropriate cells in the worksheet documentation area each time the worksheet is loaded.

Creating the \0 Macro

The documentation section of any worksheet can provide a record of who created or last worked on the data, when the worksheet was created and when it was last used.

The "Updated" portion of the documentation area of SUMMAC is completed (replaced with the current date) when the spreadsheet is exited with the Quit option from the menu. The "Created" date and "Report Date" cells have not yet been edited; the automatically executing macro, \0, will handle this task, so that each time the spreadsheet is loaded those cells will be checked and completed.

The user should be able to see this process taking place. The spreadsheet will load with the cell pointer in the same position it was when the worksheet was last saved. This may or may not be the Home position and the documentation area may or may not be visible. It would be useful to return the cell pointer to the Home position each time the spreadsheet is loaded. Therefore, the first command in the \0 macro should position the cell pointer in cell A1:

{HOME}

Now the "Created" cell needs to be checked. If this is the first time this spreadsheet was loaded, that cell would be blank and should be completed with the current date. If the worksheet had been previously created, the "Created" date would already have been entered and we would not want to change it. We must design the macro to evaluate that cell and continue processing after making a decision about what to do.

IF the "Created" date cell is *NOT* blank, *THEN* that cell should not be changed, and the macro should continue processing somewhere else—it should enter the current date in cell F7.

IF the "Created" date cell is blank, *THEN* today's date should be inserted as the "Created" date, and then the current date should be entered in cell F7.

The macro command:

{IF condition}{action}
{alternate action}

enables this decision-making process. *IF* the condition is *TRUE* (in this case, *IF* the cell is not blank, that is, the date in that cell has a value greater than 0) *THEN* macro processing continues with the action (enter the current date in the "Report Date" cell, F7, with the @NOW function).

{IF G2>0}{LET F7,@NOW}

IF the condition is *NOT TRUE*—if the value of cell G2 is 0—*THEN* the macro looks down to the next contiguous cell to find out what to do. Here the alternate action is to insert the current date in the "Created" date cell and then insert the current date in the "Report Date" cell.

{LET G2,@NOW}{LET F7,@NOW}

If these steps are contained in the \0 macro, then each time the worksheet is loaded, the "Created" date will be evaluated and the proper action taken. The current date will be entered in the "Report Date" location. When the spreadsheet is exited through the Quit option of the menu, the "Updated" date is made current. Thus completion of the spreadsheet documentation area is totally automatic.

One further automatic task would be useful to include in the \0 macro—displaying an instruction for invoking the menu. If that instruction could appear, remain visible long enough to be read, then disappear, it would not need to become a permanent part of the worksheet. The \0 macro can be instructed to branch to another macro that would contain these instructions.

The instruction "Type [Alt][M] to display the menu" can be positioned in an appropriate cell with the {LET} command:

{LET C1,Type [Alt][M] to display the menu}~

The {WAIT time} command causes 1-2-3 to halt execution and display the WAIT indicator in the upper right corner until the specified time is reached. We can have the macro pause until 5 seconds from NOW by entering the command:

{WAIT @NOW+@TIME(0,0,5)}

The (0,0,5) refers to zero hours, zero minutes, 5 seconds added to the time which is returned from the @NOW function.

When 5 seconds are over—when the TIME is 5 seconds from NOW—the next command will tell 1-2-3 what to do:

/REC1[R]

that is, erase the contents of the range C1 (our instruction cell).

Written as a macro command it becomes:

'/REC1~

If the commands to produce the instruction, wait 5 seconds, then erase the instruction are contained in a macro called \I, then we can command our \0 macro to branch to \I after it finishes taking care of the documentation.

The full \0 auto-executing macro is:

```
{HOME}
{IF G2>0}{LET F7,@NOW}{BRANCH \I}
{LET G2,@NOW}{LET F7,@NOW}{BRANCH \I}
```

The branch macro, \I is:

```
{LET C1,Type [Alt][M] to display the menu.}~
{WAIT @NOW+@TIME(0,0,5)}
'/REC1~
```

A \0 macro cannot be called by typing [Alt][0]. It only executes automatically. Therefore in order to test this macro you must either name it something else first, or save the worksheet which contains it, then retrieve that worksheet again.

Activity 11-1: Creating the \0 Macro

	Procedure	
Task	**Cell Location**	**Enter**

Create and name the \0 and \I
macros as they appear below.
Note that there are NO SPACES
between bracketed commands.

M	N	O	P
92\0	{HOME}		
93	{IF G2>0}{LET F7,@NOW}{BRANCH \I}		
94	{LET G2, @NOW}{LET F7, @NOW}{BRANCH \I}		
95			
96\I	{LET C1,Type [Alt] [M] to display the menu.}~		
97	{WAIT @NOW+@TIME(0,0,5)}		
98	/REC1~		

Save and update the worksheet by
exiting through the menu.   [Alt] [M]

Re-enter Lotus and test the \0
macro by retrieving SUMMAC.

On Your Own: Auto-executing Macro Menu

Task

Modify the Auto123 file you created in Unit X so that the menu
displays automatically when the file is loaded.

UNIT ·12·

Advanced Range Commands

Overview: Lotus 1-2-3 Release 2 has several additional range commands that make moving and copying data much easier. This unit will explore several of the advanced range commands.

Skills: Creating a table of named ranges

Transposing ranges

Converting ranges to values

Ranges can be designated by entering the coordinates of the upper left and lower right boundaries, for example, A1..E6, or by using the cell pointer to "point" to these coordinates thus visually "painting" the range. If a range is to be referred to repeatedly, it can be named and its name used in place of reentering the defining coordinates. Refer to the material in Unit VI on naming ranges.

Range names can be used whenever a prompt requests a group of cells to act on, for example, in the MOVE, COPY, or ERASE command. Range names can replace specified ranges in formulas and functions, for example, @AVG(AGE). In addition, named ranges can be extracted from (copied out of) a spreadsheet to a new worksheet, or combined with (read into) the current worksheet.

Besides RANGE NAME, there are other Lotus commands that specifically act on cell ranges. The UNPROTECT and PROTECT commands restrict access to specified ranges. The RANGE VALUE command converts a range from formulas to values to facilitate manipulation of data containing formulas within a spreadsheet. The RANGE TRANSPOSE command allows converting rows to columns and vice versa. In this unit, you will explore the use of these range commands.

Activity 12-1: Naming Ranges

Note: Use your macro library in the following units by file combining it into the spreadsheet on which you are working. You will need to rename your macros after a File Combine. Another way to proceed is to use the MACTEMP or AUTO123 files you made containing the macro library, file combining the new file into it. You may need to change column widths and formats. See Unit X.

| | | Procedure | |
Task	Cell Location	Enter	
Load the spreadsheet, EMPLOYEE, and examine its contents.		/FR EMPLOYEE [R]	
FILE COMBINE MACLIB into an unused part of the spreadsheet; name ranges. See Unit X if you need help.			
There are several potential ranges which we may want to work with in this course. Use the RANGE NAME CREATE command to name the ranges for REVIEW and RANK.	G6	/RNC REVIEW [R] [End] [Down] [R]	
	H6	/RNC RANK [R] [End] [Down] [R]	
Name the range HIREDATE on your own.			

	Procedure	
Task	**Cell Location**	**Enter**
You may also name ranges that contain no data; however, you cannot use [End] [Down] to define the range.	I6	/RNC SALARY [R] I6..I19 [R] or point

Name these additional ranges:

AGE	L6..L19
YRS_EMPL	M6..M19
WKS_VAC	N6..N19
BONUS	O6..O19

Tip: You may wish to keep spreadsheet range names separate from macro range names in the titles list. You may do so by beginning the name with a number or character such as the asterisk.

Activity 12-2: Creating a Table of Named Ranges

Once you have named several ranges, you can create a table to document your work.

	Procedure	
Task	**Cell Location**	**Enter**
Position the cell pointer in an unused portion of the worksheet and enter a title.	B30	RANGE NAMES [R]
Create the table and accept B32 as the starting point of the range.	B32	/RNT [R]
Name the table.	B30	/RNC RANGE NAMES [R]
Accept B30 as start of range.		[R]
Goto A1 and quickly locate your table.		[Home] [F5] RANGE NAMES [R]
You may also use the Name Key, [F3], to recall a named range.		[F5] [F3] RANGE NAMES [R]
Save your spreadsheet.		[Alt] [S]

The RANGE TRANSPOSE Command

The RANGE TRANSPOSE command reorders a range from columns to rows and vice versa. A copy of the original range is transposed to another area of the spreadsheet leaving the copied range intact. It is not possible to transpose a range onto itself. If the range to be transposed contains relative formulas, they must be made absolute or converted to values if they are to be transposed correctly.

Activity 12-3: Transposing Ranges

In this activity, you will transpose labels and values in the SALES file. Labels will be transposed directly while data will be converted prior to transposing via the RANGE VALUE command.

		Procedure
Task	Cell Location	Enter
Retrieve the file SALES.		/FR SALES [R]
FILE COMBINE MACLIB.		
Enter a new title in C12.	C12	SALES DATA BY REGION [R]
Position the pointer on the first row heading.	A4	
Transpose the column headings to A14.	A4	/RT A4..G4 [R] A14 [R]
Transpose the row headings to B14.	A5	/RT A5..A8 [R] B14 [R]
Transpose the data table to B15.	B5	/RT B5..G8 [R] B15 [R]

Note: What happened to the transposed formulas?

The RANGE VALUE Command

The RANGE VALUE command converts formulas to their numeric value. Ranges can be converted to the same area of the spreadsheet; however, the original formulas will be overwritten.

Activity 12-4: Converting Formulas to Values

		Procedure	
Task	**Cell Location**	**Enter**	
RANGE NAME the data in F5..G8 STATS.	F5	/RNCSTATS [R] F5..G8 [R]	
Convert the data to values.	F5	/RVSTATS [R] STATS [R]	
Transpose this range into the new table.	F5	/RTSTATS [R] B19..E20 [R]	
Save the file.		[Alt] [S]	

Note: If you wish to retain the formulas, write the values to a different location on the spreadsheet.

	A	B	C	D	E	F	G
1			SALES DATA BY QUARTER				
2							
3							
4		JAN-MAR	APR-JUNE	JULY-SEPT	OCT-DEC	TOTALS	AVERAGES
5	NORTH	33854.00	34699.00	35732.00	32876.00	137161.00	34290.25
6	SOUTH	31677.00	30428.00	29533.00	28955.00	120593.00	30148.25
7	EAST	25478.00	26377.00	27198.00	27850.00	106903.00	26725.75
8	WEST	45788.00	45900.00	43877.00	45933.00	181498.00	45374.50
9							
10							
11							
12			SALES DATA BY REGION				
13							
14		NORTH	SOUTH	EAST	WEST		
15	JAN-MAR	33854.00	31677.00	25478.00	45788.00		
16	APR-JUNE	34699.00	30428.00	26377.00	45900.00		
17	JULY-SEPT	35732.00	29533.00	27198.00	43877.00		
18	OCT-DEC	32876.00	28955.00	27850.00	45933.00		
19	TOTALS	137161.00	120593.00	106903.00	181498.00		
20	AVERAGES	34290.25	30148.25	26725.75	45374.50		

On Your Own: RANGE PROTECT

1. Try RANGE PROTECT on B19..E20.

2. After you issue the command, try to RANGE ERASE B19..E20 to see whether the command worked.

3. Use [F1] to find out how to remedy the situation.

4. Restore the data, correct, and test.

5. UNPROTECT the range.

UNIT ·13·

Lotus 1-2-3 Functions

Overview: Lotus 1-2-3 contains a whole range of functions that allow you to create additional data from existing data and view data in many different ways. In this unit, you will explore five groups of Lotus functions including CALENDAR, LOGICAL, SPECIAL, STATISTICAL, and DATABASE STATISTICAL that will expand your capability to analyze spreadsheet data.

Skills: Understanding Lotus 1-2-3 functions

Using calendar functions and date arithmetic

Selecting from two alternatives — @IF

Selecting from a list — @CHOOSE

Constructing a Lookup table

Using @VLOOKUP

Applying mathematical and statistical functions

Using database statistical functions

What Functions Are

Functions are tools that perform spreadsheet tasks such as:

* Substitute for mathematical, statistical, or financial formulas.

* Perform mathematics using dates.

* Perform error checking.

* Make selections from two or more choices.

The Syntax of Functions

Lotus 1-2-3's automated functions are composed of the following parts:

SYNTAX: @NAME(data)

EXAMPLE: @SUM(B1..B10)

Part	Explanation
@	Distinguishes the name of the function from other text entries such as labels and range names.
NAME	Represents the name of the function. It is generally some-what descriptive of its use. For example, @SUM adds the data indicated between the parentheses.
( )	Mark the beginning and end of the data on which the function operates.
data	The values on which a function acts. The data is also referred to as the "Argument" of the function.

Data items within the parentheses are separated when necessary by commas. The data on which functions act may include digits (5,6,7), formulas (7+8), contents of cells identified by location (B1..B10), contents of cells identified by range names (TOTALS), logical expressions (3>4), and/or a combination of any of these.

The Calendar Functions

While the format in which you record dates and times is easy to understand, it does not lend itself to mathematical manipulation. Lotus 1-2-3 is one of the first programs to automate the process of doing mathematics with calendar information.

Lotus provides many functions which facilitate the manipulation of date type information. They are:

Function	Explanation
@NOW	Returns serial number of current date and time.
@DATE(yy,mm,dd)	Returns serial date number.
@DATEVALUE("date string")	Returns serial date number.
@DAY(date number)	Returns day of month of date number.

@MONTH   Returns month of date number.

@YEAR   Returns year of date number.

@MOD(@DATE(yy,mm,dd),7)   Returns the day of the week for a
                                given date {Sat=0, Sun=1, etc.}.

Using Date Functions to Automate a Database

The @NOW function is used to display the system date and time in
the cell location in which the function is typed. It is recorded as a
Julian calendar (serial) date.

A Julian calendar date is a number that represents the number of days
a particular date is from January 1, 1900. 1-2-3's date functions convert
the month, day, year format that you use into equivalent Julian calendar
values. It is the fact that Julian calendar dates are a continuous sequence
of numbers which makes possible their use in arithmetic operations.

Like the @NOW function the @DATE function yields serial values.
The format in which the @DATE function is written is shown below.

@DATE(yy,mm,dd) where:

  yy = last two digits of year
mm = month
  dd = day

Activity 13-1: Entering Date Functions

In a spreadsheet containing personnel records you will perform the following tasks:

- Record today's date using the @NOW function.
- Create formulas that reference today's date to calculate the age of each employee and the years of employment:

Employee Age = (@Now - Birthdate)/365
Years Employed = (@Now - Hiredate)/365

		Procedure	
Task	Cell Location	Enter	
Retrieve the file EMPLOYEE.			
FILE COMBINE MACLIB.			
Enter the date as a serial number.	C1	@NOW	
Format the date entry to DATE FORMAT 1.	C1	[Alt] [Y]	
Position the screen.		[F5] J1	
Move pointer to first entry in AGE column.	L6		
Enter the formula to calculate the current age of each employee.	L6	(@NOW-K6)/365	
Enter the formula to calculate the years employed.	M6	(@NOW-J6)/365	
Copy the formulas down the columns.	L6	/C L6..M6 [R] L7..L19 [R]	
Format the AGE column to Fixed, 0 decimals; the YRS EMPL to Fixed, 1 decimal.	L6 M6	[Alt] [F] 0 [R] [Alt] [F] 1 [R]	

Spreadsheet Reflecting Date Arithmetic and Reformatting

	H	I	J	K	L	M	N
	RANK	SALARY	HIREDATE	BIRTHDATE	AGE	YRS_EMPL	WKS_VAC
1							
2							
3							
4							
5	RANK	SALARY	HIREDATE	BIRTHDATE	AGE	YRS_EMPL	WKS_VAC
6	17		25-Jan-80	03-Dec-41	47	8.5	
7	14		12-Mar-61	02-Dec-30	58	27.4	
8	16		13-Dec-83	02-Feb-40	48	4.6	
9	13		14-Jun-84	09-May-54	34	4.1	
10	13		23-Oct-86	07-Aug-62	26	1.7	
11	16		03-Feb-75	08-Nov-55	33	13.5	
12	14		30-Apr-84	16-Sep-55	33	4.2	
13	13		09-Nov-81	07-Sep-56	32	6.7	
14	12		25-Nov-87	05-Apr-62	26	0.6	
15	14		25-Feb-83	04-Dec-59	29	5.4	
16	13		12-May-87	30-Jun-63	25	1.2	
17	16		25-Jun-73	13-Mar-44	44	15.1	
18	13		13-Feb-86	08-Sep-60	28	2.4	
19	16		21-Dec-87	25-Jan-60	28	0.6	

Logical and Special Functions

The Logical and Special Functions to be covered in the activities that follow are ones that allow you to build conditional tests into the spreadsheet. These tests are usually used to make a selection between two or more choices.

FUNCTION	MEANING
@IF	To select from two alternatives
@CHOOSE	To select from a short list
@VLOOKUP	To select from a vertical table
@HLOOKUP	To select from a horizontal table

Selection from Two Alternatives—@IF(A,Rtrue,Rfalse)

When a selection is to be made between two alternatives use the @IF function. It evaluates a condition for its truth or falseness and allows you to select one of two actions based upon the result.

@IF can be used to evaluate items that 1-2-3 regards as values (digits, formulas, functions, or references to cells that contain one of these), or items that 1-2-3 regards as labels if these items are enclosed in quotation marks.

This function has the following general syntax (structure):

```
SYNTAX:    @IF(a,rtrue,rfalse)

EXAMPLE:   @IF(C1=0,@NOW,C1)
```

Where:

a   Represents the condition (expression) to be evaluated for its truth or falseness.

rtrue   Represents the result if the condition evaluates as true.

rfalse   Represents the result if the condition evaluates to false.

And the meaning can be interpreted as follows:

If a is true, then display the expression represented by rtrue, otherwise display the expression represented by rfalse.

If C1 contains 0, then display the system date, otherwise display the value in C1.

Evaluating the Expression—Relational Operators

The conditions that are evaluated in the @IF function require the use of relational operators. Relational operators are symbols that show the relationship between two values.

Operator	Relationship
=	Equal
<	Less than
<=	Less than or equal to
>	Greater than
>=	Greater than or equal to
<>	Not equal

All relationships between values are either true or false. For example 7>3 is clearly true, 5<4 is false. You can use these relationships within the @IF function to select a course of action. For example:

@IF(C2>C1,0,1) means if the value in cell C2 is greater than the value in C1 then display 0 here, or else display 1.

Activity 13-2: Using @IF

You will use this knowledge to test whether the date of the last update is within 30 days by testing whether it is less than today's date minus 30.

Task	Procedure Cell Location	Enter
Position the pointer.	A1	
Enter the @IF function below to determine if the spreadsheet has been updated.	C3	
@IF(C2>C1-30,"Updated","Not Updated")		
Save your spreadsheet.		[Alt] [S]

Evaluating the Expression—Logical Operators

Test conditions may be made more specific through the use of the logical operators such as:

Operator	Meaning
#NOT#	Not
#AND#	And
#OR#	Or

You will use the logical operator #AND# to test whether the date of the last update is greater than 30 days prior to today's date *AND* whether it is greater than or equal to the beginning of the fiscal year, January 1, 1988.

Activity 13.3: Using Logical Operators with @IF

		Procedure	
Task		**Cell Location**	**Enter**
Position the pointer.		C3	

Enter the function below:

@IF(C2>C1-30#AND#C2>=@DATE(88,1,1),"Updated","Not Updated")

Since you just updated the spreadsheet, edit the date in C2. Notice that the @IF function immediately reflects the new condition.

Selection from a List—@CHOOSE(Key,A1,A2..An)

The @CHOOSE function is designed to make a selection from a reasonably short list of choices. Longer lists are generally placed in tables. The function has the following form:

SYNTAX: @CHOOSE(key, argument, ... argument)

EXAMPLE: @CHOOSE(C3, 51, 39, 73, 79, ...,5)

Where:

Key   Is a value which represents the position of the argument
             to be selected relative to the first argument in the list.
             (For example, if the value in C3 is 0 the number 51 is
             chosen for display, if C3 equals 1 the number 39 is
             chosen for display, and so on.)

Argument   Represents a value or string that is selected from the list
             and displayed when its position in the list corresponds to
             the position indicated by the key.

The key in the @CHOOSE function may be any data that 1-2-3 regards as values (digits, formulas, functions), or references to locations which contain them. The arguments may be any value or string enclosed in parentheses.

Activity 13-4: Exploring @CHOOSE

You will try a few examples before applying @CHOOSE to your database problem.

Task	Procedure Cell Location	Enter
Position the pointer.	P1	

Enter the @CHOOSE function below in P1:

@CHOOSE(0,100,200,250,400,500)

The value 100 is displayed because the key of 0 directs the function to display argument 0, which is a 100.

QUESTION: What value will be displayed if the key is changed to 4? Try it!

Position the pointer.	P2	

Enter the @CHOOSE function below:

@CHOOSE(Q1,"ADMIN","PURCH","PERSN","BUDGT","LEGAL","ACCTG","CLRCL")

ADMIN is displayed because Q1 is empty and therefore 0, so the key is the same as the previous example and the 0 offset is selected.

Position the pointer.	Q1	
Enter a value.		3

Notice that P2 now displays BUDGT as directed by the new value of the key Q1.

Task	Procedure Cell Location	Enter
Position the pointer.	P3	
Enter the function.		@IF(Q1>5,5,Q1)

Because the value in Q1 is not greater
than 5, the second alternative, the
value in Q1, is displayed.

| Change the value in Q1. | Q1 | 6 |

Note the immediate update.

Activity 13-5: Using @CHOOSE in Database Management

An annual employee bonus is awarded based on the length of service
to the company. To determine this bonus, years of service are divided
by 5 and a bonus awarded on the basis of the resulting figure. The
@CHOOSE function will handle this task. Those employees working less
than 5 years will have a key value of 0, e.g., 3/5=0, and will receive the
first value in the function's argument list.

Task	Procedure Cell Location	Enter
Clear the work area.		/RE P1.Q4 [R]
Position the pointer.	O6	

Enter the formula as it appears below:

@CHOOSE((M6/5),100,250,500,750,1000,"TRIP")

Copy the formula from O7 through O19.	O6	/C [R] O7..O19 [R]
Examine the results.		
Save your spreadsheet.		[Alt] [S]

Activity 13-6: Combining @IF with @CHOOSE

The length of employment is often a factor in determining the number of weeks paid vacation to which an employee is entitled. You will use the @CHOOSE function along with the @IF function to automate the updating of the vacation time as the years in service increase.

The results should satisfy the following vacation rule. All employees working fewer than 5 years and more than 1 year receive vacation as a direct relationship to their years of employment, for example, an employee working 3.4 years will get 3 weeks vacation. All employees working five years or more receive 6 weeks vacation. Employees working less than 1 year receive no vacation.

The @IF portion of the formula determines the key for the @CHOOSE function. If employees have worked more than 5 years, they will have a key of 5. Applying this to the @CHOOSE function will return the 5th argument, 6. Remember, the arguments are numbered beginning at zero since it is actually an offset from the beginning of the list.

	Procedure	
Task	**Cell Location**	**Enter**
Position the pointer.	N6	
Enter the formula below:		
@CHOOSE((@IF(M6>=5,5,M6)),0,1,2,3,4,6)		
Copy the formula down the column.	N6	/C [R]
		N7..N19 [R]
Save your spreadsheet.		[Alt] [S]

Spreadsheet Reflecting @IF and @CHOOSE Functions

	J	K	L	M	N	O
1						
2						
3						
4						
5	HIREDATE	BIRTHDATE	AGE	YRS_EMPL	WKS_VAC	BONUS
6	25-Jan-80	03-Dec-41	47	8.5	6	250
7	12-Mar-61	02-Dec-30	58	27.4	6	TRIP
8	13-Dec-83	02-Feb-40	48	4.6	4	100
9	14-Jun-84	09-May-54	34	4.2	4	100
10	23-Oct-86	07-Aug-62	26	1.7	1	100
11	03-Feb-75	08-Nov-55	33	13.5	6	500
12	30-Apr-84	16-Sep-55	33	4.2	4	100
13	09-Nov-81	07-Sep-56	32	6.7	6	250
14	25-Nov-87	05-Apr-62	26	0.6	0	100
15	25-Feb-83	04-Dec-59	29	5.4	6	250
16	12-May-87	30-Jun-63	25	1.2	1	100
17	25-Jun-73	13-Mar-44	44	15.1	6	750
18	13-Feb-86	08-Sep-60	28	2.4	2	100
19	21-Dec-87	25-Jan-60	28	0.6	0	100

Selecting from Tables—@VLOOKUP @HLOOKUP

The lookup functions are used to locate a value in either a vertical or horizontal table. The table must consist of two or more adjacent rows or columns. The first column or row contains comparison values to be used to look up the corresponding data in the adjacent rows or columns. Her is an example of a two-column vertical table:

```
+-----------------------------------+
|            Salary Table           |
|                                   |
|     Rank           Salary         |
|      12            25000          |
|      13            35000          |
|      14            45000          |
|      15            55000          |
|      16            65000          |
|      17            75000          |
+-----------------------------------+
```

Given the rank of an employee, one can quickly identify the appropriate salary level by finding the rank in the left hand column and looking one column to the right for the salary. 1-2-3 automates this lookup procedure with its @VLOOKUP function.

Activity 13-7: Constructing a Lookup Table

Continuing the process of completing the EMPLOYEE spreadsheet, you want to use the employees' job rank to lookup and enter the employees' salaries in column I of the spreadsheet. When job rank changes the salary column will be automatically updated. The @VLOOKUP function is just the tool to accomplish this goal.

The first step in creating a table is simply entering the table of data from which the lookup will be performed. On a blank area of the spreadsheet you will construct a table of job ranks with corresponding salaries.

	Procedure	
Task	**Cell Location**	**Enter**
Position the pointer.	J30	
Enter the labels shown below.		
Move to the data area.	J34	
On your own, create the table using Data Fill. (See UNIT VII.)		
Name the range J34..K39 LOOKUP TABLE.	J34	/RNC LOOKUP TABLE [R] J34..K39 [R]
Save your spreadsheet.		[Alt] [S]

	I	J	K
28			
29	**		
30		SALARY LOOKUP	
31		TABLE	
32			
33		RANK	SALARY
34		12	25000
35		13	35000
36		14	45000
37		15	55000
38		16	65000
39		17	75000

Selection Using @VLOOKUP—@VLOOKUP (Key, Table Range, Column Offset)

Now that the table is entered you can write the @VLOOKUP function. The function is entered in the cell in which you want the result displayed. Its general syntax is as follows:

```
SYNTAX:   @VLOOKUP(key, table range, column offset)

EXAMPLE:  @VLOOKUP(12, P7, Q12, 1)
```

Where:

Key — Represents the value to be looked up. It may be a digit, formula, function or cell reference.

Table range — Represents the location of the table including the column with key values and the columns containing the values to be looked up.

Column offset — Represents how many columns the values to be looked up are from the column containing the key. An offset of 1 indicates the first column to the right of the key.

The function above can be interpreted as follows:

In a vertical table located in the range from P7 to Q12, lookup the value 12 and display the value from the column 1 to the right.

Activity 13-8: Using @VLOOKUP with Data Tables

In this activity you will go to the salary column and enter the lookup function referencing job rank as the key to lookup. Using absolute cell referencing (for copying later) enter the location of the table you created as the table range and set the column offset to 1. Copy this function down column I to record each employee's salary.

	Procedure	
Task	**Cell Location**	**Enter**
Position the screen.		[F5] H1 [R]
Position the pointer.	I6	
Enter the following function:		
@VLOOKUP(H6,$LOOKUP TABLE,1)		
Copy the function down the column to I19.	I6	/C [R] I7..I19 [R]
Format the SALARY field to Currency (no decimals) format and save the spreadsheet.	I6	/RFCO [R] I6..I19 [R] [Alt] [S]

Your salary data should match the table shown below.

I6: (C0) [W8] @VLOOKUP(H6,$LOOKUP TABLE,1)

	I	J	K
4			
5	SALARY	HIREDATE	BIRTHDATE
6	$75,000	25-Jan-80	03-Dec-41
7	$45,000	12-Mar-61	02-Dec-30
8	$65,000	13-Dec-83	02-Feb-40
9	$35,000	14-Jun-84	09-May-54
10	$35,000	23-Oct-86	07-Aug-62
11	$65,000	03-Feb-75	08-Nov-55
12	$45,000	30-Apr-84	16-Sep-55
13	$35,000	09-Nov-81	07-Sep-56
14	$25,000	25-Nov-87	05-Apr-62
15	$45,000	25-Feb-83	04-Dec-59
16	$35,000	12-May-87	30-Jun-63
17	$65,000	25-Jun-73	13-Mar-44
18	$35,000	13-Feb-86	08-Sep-60
19	$65,000	21-Dec-87	25-Jan-60

Lotus Statistical Functions

The following functions are available to you when working with spreadsheet data:

Function	Explanation
@SUM	Computes the total of all values in a cell range.
@COUNT	Returns the number of entries in a range.
@MIN	Returns the minimum value in a range.
@MAX	Returns the maximum value in a range.
@AVG	Computes the average of a range.
@SQRT	Computes the square root of a cell entry.
@ROUND	Rounds a cell entry to a specified number of digits.
@INT	Returns the integer portion of an entry.
@ABS	Returns the absolute value of an entry.
@RAND	Generates a random number.
@MOD	Returns the remainder from division.
@PI	Returns the value of pi to 15 decimal places.

Activity 13-9: Applying Statistical Functions

	Procedure	
Task	**Cell Location**	**Enter**
Review the data in the spreadsheet EMPLOYEE.		
Generate the table of statistical data shown below by entering labels.	J21	STATISTICAL SUMMARY
	E24	AVERAGE
	E25	MINIMUM
	E26	MAXIMUM
Copy the headings from G5..N5 to G23..N23.	G5	/CG5..N5 [R]
		G23 [R]
Enter the statistical functions for the REVIEW column.	G24	@AVG(REVIEW)
	G25	@MIN(REVIEW)
	G26	@MAX(REVIEW)
On your own, copy the range G24..G26 across the spreadsheet from H24 to N26.		
Format the table to Fixed, 0 decimals, and the two date columns to Date 1.	G24	/RFF0 [R]
		G24..N26 [R]
	J24	[Alt] [Y]
	K24	[Alt] [Y]
Save the spreadsheet.		[Alt] [S]

	E	F	G	H	I	J	K	L	M	N
20										
21						STATISTICAL SUMMARY				
22										
23			REVIEW	RANK	SALARY	HIREDATE	BIRTHDATE	AGE	YRS_EMPL	WKS_VAC
24	AVERAGE		89	14	47857	10-Sep-81	25-Jun-53	35	7	4
25	MINIMUM		56	12	25000	12-Mar-61	02-Feb-30	25	1	0
26	MAXIMUM		98	17	75000	21-Dec-87	30-Jun-63	58	27	6

Statistical Functions for Database Analysis

1-2-3 has a number of statistical functions that are used specifically to facilitate analysis of spreadsheet data maintained in database format. These functions utilize selection criteria to analyze data in database fields. They include the following:

FUNCTION	MEANING
@DCOUNT	Counts the number of items in a list
@DAVG	Gives the average of values in a list
@DMIN	Gives the minimum value in a list
@DMAX	Gives the maximum value in a list
@DSTD	Gives the standard deviation
@DVAR	Gives the varience

Format of Functions for Database Analysis

All of the database statistical functions are written in the general format which follows:

@DFUNCT(Input range, column offset, Criterion range)

Where:

DFUNC   Represents the name of the function.

Input range   Identifies the area of the worksheet in which the database in located.

Column offset   Identifies the field in the database on which the function will operate. A value of zero indicates the first column: a 1 indicates the second column, etc.

Criterion range   Identifies the area of the worksheet which contains the description of the records to be selected for inclusion in the analysis.

Counting Selected Records in a Database

The @DCOUNT function can be used to count the number of individuals in a database who fit a specified description.

Establishing the selection criteria is essential prior to using any of the database functions. A format for displaying both the criteria and output ranges has been established for you on the student disk.

In the following Activity, you will FILE COMBINE this format into your worksheet and use the @DCOUNT function to count the number of employees who earn over $45,000. In addition, you will be able to calculate the percent of individuals meeting particular criteria in that salary category.

Activity 13-10: Using @DCOUNT

	Procedure	
Task	**Cell Location**	**Enter**
Position the pointer.		[F5] R1 [R]
FILE COMBINE the entire contents of the file DSTATS.		/FCCE DSTATS [R]
Specify the criteria for both salary and gender in the designated criteria ranges.	S7	+I6>=45000
	T7	+E6="F"
	S10	+I6>=45000
	T10	+E6="M"
Format the range S7..T10 to text.	S7	/RFTS7..T10 [R]
Name the entire database.	A5	/RNC DATABASE [R] A5..O19 [R]

Task	Procedure Cell Location	Enter
Enter the @DCOUNT function into the appropriate cells.	X7	@DCOUNT ($DATABASE, 4,S6..T7)
	X9	@DCOUNT ($DATABASE, 4,S9..T10)
To compute the percent, divide the count in X7 and X9 by the total number of females and males respectively.	X8	+X7/ @DCOUNT ($DATABASE, 4,T6..T7)
	X10	+X9/ @DCOUNT ($DATABASE, 4,T9..T10)

On your own, format the percent results to percent with no decimal places.

Using @DAVG, @DMAX, and @DMIN

Additional database statistical functions can give you further information about the characteristics of your database. The difference between these functions and the Lotus functions @AVG, @MIN, and @MAX is that you can select records meeting certain criteria to be acted on by the functions. The non- database functions act on a simple range of numbers only.

Activity 13-11: Using @DAVG, @DMAX, @DMIN

Task	Procedure Cell Location	Enter
Enter the functions to generate the statistics on the entire database.	AB8	@DAVG($DATABASE, 11,T6..T10)
	AB9	@DMAX($DATABASE, 11,T6..T10)
	AB10	@DMIN($DATABASE, 11,T6..T10)
Enter the functions to generate the statistics on only those employees making over $45,000.	AC8	@DAVG($DATABASE, 11,S6..S7)
	AC9	@DMAX($DATABASE, 11,S6..S7)
	AC10	@DMIN($DATABASE, 11,S6..S7)

On your own, format AB8..AC10 to Fixed, 0 decimals.

Save your spreadsheet.

Compare your statistics to those shown below.

```
    R        S         T      U V W        X     Y  Z    AA    AB       AC
1   ---------------------------------------------------------------------
2   |                        |                                          |
3   | CRITERION AREA         |          STATISTICS                      |
4   |                        |                                          |
5   |                        | Making over $45,000 | Employee Age Data  |
6   | SALARY     GENDER      |                     |                     |
7   | +I6>=45000 +E6="F"     | T. Female      4    |         All   >=$45 |
8   |                        | % Female      57%   | Avg Age   35    40  |
9   | SALARY     GENDER      | T. Male        4    | Max Age   58    58  |
10  | +I6>=45000 +E6="M"     | % Male        57%   | Min Age   25    29  |
11  |                        |                     |                     |
12  |                        |                     |                     |
13  |_____|_____|_____|
```

Note: Your age data will differ from the above.

On Your Own: Functions

1. How many Code 3 persons were hired on or after January 1, 1985?

2. What percentage of the total number of Code 3 persons is it?

Case Study #4: Functions

The company policy is to offer an incentive for cash payment, especially of smaller amounts. The following discounts are offered:

10% for amounts from $100 to $500.

5% for amounts from $500 to $5,000.

3% for amounts from $5,000 to $10,000.

Use the lookup function to calculate the discount and net on cash sales of:

$5,656.52

$7,450.29

$186.00

$52,778.97

UNIT·14·

*Lotus Financial Functions
and Data Tables*

Overview: In working with the payment financial function, @PMT, you will gain additional experience in ways of building and using Lotus 1-2-3 functions. You will also see how data tables are constructed based on first one and then two variables contained in the @PMT function.

Skills: Building a function

Variations on the @PMT function

    Values

    Cell references

    Range names

Creating data tables with one and two variables

The Financial Functions

Lotus has five functions that are used to provide built-in financial calculations. These are used in business to study the values of investments from a variety of perspectives.

FUNCTION	MEANING
@PMT	PAYMENT
@PV	PRESENT VALUE
@FV	FUTURE VALUE
@NPV	NET PRESENT VALUE
@IRR	INTERNAL RATE OF RETURN

The Payment Function—@PMT(Principal,Interest,Term)

The @PMT function is used to calculate the amount of a periodic payment on a loan. Given the principal, interest rate per payment period, and number of payment periods, this function will display the amount of the periodic payment in the cell in which the function is located.

The function is written as follows:

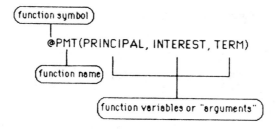

Where:

Principal   Refers to the amount of money to be borrowed.

Interest   Refers to the interest rate per payment period (days,months,years)

Term   Refers to the number of payment periods (days, months, years).

Each argument may be entered into the function as a digit, cell reference, range name, formula, or function.

Activity 14-1: Using the Payment Function

This exercise will calculate the annual payments on an employees credit union loan principal amount of $10,000 at an interest of 5% over a term of 5 years.

Task	Procedure Cell Location	Enter
Save the current spreadsheet and clear the screen and memory.		[Alt] [S] /WEY
Set column width globally to 10.		/WGC10 [R]
Enter the @PMT function.	A1	@PMT(10000,5%,5)

Your screen will show the following:

A1: @PMT(10000,0.05,5)

```
        A        B
1   2309.7479
2
```

The use of cell references instead of values in a function offers the advantage of automatic recalculation upon the entry of a new principal, interest and/or term. Enter the labels and values shown below:

	A	B	C
1	Loan Data		
2			
3	Principal	10000	
4	Interest	0.05	
5	Term	5	
6			
7	Payment		

Like formulas, functions can be entered by typing the entire function or by a combination of typing and pointing to the cells containing the data to be used in the calculation.

	Procedure	
Task	Cell Location	Enter
Enter the @PMT function using pointing.	B7	@PMT(
Point to B3.	B3	'
Point to B4.	B4	'
Point to B5.	B5	) [R]

	A	B
1	Loan Data	
2		
3	Principal	10000
4	Interest	0.05
5	Term	5
6		
7	Payment	2309.7479

Activity 14-2: Using Range Names in the Payment Function

The use of named ranges to identify the data on which a function operates will often make its application clearer.

Using the range name command menu, give the cell locations referred to in the payment function appropriately descriptive names as follows.

		Procedure	
Task	**Cell Location**	**Enter**	
Position the pointer.	A3		
Select Range Name Labels Right.		/RNLR	
Expand pointer.	A5	[R]	
Position the cell pointer.	B7		

Your screen should look like this:

```
B7:  @PMT (PRINCIPAL, INTEREST, TERM)
        A          B        C        D
  1   Loan Data
  2
  3   Principal    10000
  4   Interest      0.05
  5   Term             5
  6
  7   Payment  2309.7479
```

On your own, format the result in B7 to currency and save this activity as PMT.

Creating Data Tables with the Payment Function

1-2-3 can automatically create tables that will show the results of the payment function for a list of different interest rates, principal amounts and/or payment periods. This feature can be used by borrowers or lenders to quickly determine the payments for a variety of different loan arrangements.

Below is a table of payments for varying interest rates. It is based upon a loan amount of $10,000 with annual payments over a term of five years.

Interest	Payment
10.0%	$2,637.97
11.0%	$2,705.70
12.0%	$2,774.10
13.0%	$2,843.15
14.0%	$2,912.84
15.0%	$2,983.16
16.0%	$3,054.09
17.0%	$3,125.64

Activity 14-3: Creating a One-Variable Data Table

The first step in creating a table is to prepare the layout on the spreadsheet from which a one-variable table can be created.

Task	Cell Location	Procedure Enter
Alter the column width of B to 30.	B1	/WCS30 [R]
Enter the labels in A11 and B11.	A11 B11	INTEREST [R] ^PAYMENT [R]
Position the pointer.	B12	
Enter the @PMT function.		@PMT (PRINCIPAL, INTEREST, TERM)

Note: You may also enter the function as @PMT (B3,B4,B5)

Format B12 to Text.	B12	/RFT [R]

On your own, format B3 to Currency, B4 to Percent, 1 decimal place, and B5 to Fixed, 1 decimal place.

B12: (T) @PMT(PRINCIPAL,INTEREST,TERM)

	A	B
1	Loan Data	
2		
3	Principal	$10,000.00
4	Interest	5.0%
5	Term	5.0
6		
7	Payment	$2,309.75
8		
9		
10		
11	INTEREST	PAYMENT
12		@PMT(PRINCIPAL,INTEREST,TERM)

In our layout the left column will contain a list of values that represent interest rates in the table. To the right, one cell above the first interest entry is the function to be calculated. Immediately below the function, payment amounts will appear upon execution of the data table command sequence.

	Procedure	
Task	**Cell Location**	**Enter**
Position the pointer.	A13	
Select the Data Fill Command.		/DFA13..A20 [R]
Enter the value to start.		10% [R]
Enter the increment.		1% [R]
Accept the stop value.		[R]

On your own, format the range to Percent, 1 decimal place.

The values displayed in A13..A20 may be used in the Table which is constructed in the exercise on the following page.

A13: (P1) 0.1

11	INTEREST	PAYMENT
12		@PMT(PRINCIPAL,INTEREST,TERM)
13	10.0%	
14	11.0%	
15	12.0%	
16	13.0%	
17	14.0%	
18	15.0%	
19	16.0%	
20	17.0%	

The layout for the table is complete. You need only identify the location of the table along with its input cell to have the table of payments automatically calculated. The picture below illustrates the information to be identified to execute the data table.

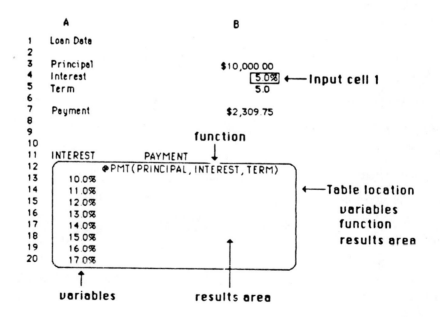

Where:

Table location	Is a range which includes within its borders the column of values to substitute into the function, the function, and the area in which the results are to be written.
Input cell	Is the argument in the function which is represented by the values in the left column of the table.

Activity 14-4: Using the DATA TABLE Command to Generate a Table

The identification is performed through the data table command menus as illustrated in the following exercise. At the conclusion of this command sequence the payments will be calculated and displayed in column B.

The input cell is the argument in the function which is represented by the values in the left column of the table. In this example the argument represented is the interest rate.

The input cell is identified during the table command by referencing the location indicated in the function. In this example that location is the range named INTEREST.

	Procedure	
Task	**Cell Location**	**Enter**
Position the pointer.	A12	
Select the Data Table Command.		/DT1A12..B20 [R]
Press the Name key.		[F3]
Select INTEREST.		INTEREST [R]

On your own, format B13..B20 to
Currency, 2 decimal places.

	A	B	C
11	INTEREST	PAYMENT	
12		@PMT(PRINCIPAL,INTEREST,TERM)	
13	10.0%	$2,637.97	
14	11.0%	$2,705.70	
15	12.0%	$2,774.10	
16	13.0%	$2,843.15	
17	14.0%	$2,912.84	
18	15.0%	$2,983.16	
19	16.0%	$3,054.09	
20	17.0%	$3,125.64	

Creating a Two-Variable Data Table

1-2-3 also has the capability to produce a table based upon two variables.

In the exercise which follows you will create a table to compute the annual payments on loans with a term of five years for a variety of interest rates and principal amounts.

The resulting table should look like the one below:

PAYMENT TABLE
(Interest from 10.0% - 17.0%)
(Principal from $8,000 to $12,000)

	$8,000.00	$9,000.00	$10,000.00	$11,000.00	$12,000.00
10.0%	2,110.38	2,374.18	2,637.97	2,901.77	3,165.57
11.0%	2,164.56	2,435.13	2,705.70	2,976.27	3,246.84
12.0%	2,219.28	2,496.69	2,774.10	3,051.51	3,328.92
13.0%	2,274.52	2,558.83	2,843.15	3,127.46	3,411.77
14.0%	2,330.27	2,621.55	2,912.84	3,204.12	3,495.40
15.0%	2,386.52	2,684.84	2,983.16	3,281.47	3,579.79
16.0%	2,443.28	2,748.68	3,054.09	3,359.50	3,664.91
17.0%	2,500.51	2,813.07	3,125.64	3,438.20	3,750.77

Activity 14-5: Creating a Two-Variable Data Table

	Procedure	
Task	**Cell Location**	**Enter**

Save the spreadsheet as TABLE1.

Retrieve TABLE.

Your screen already contains the layout for a two-variable table and should resemble the screen below.

	A	B	C	D	E	F
8			PAYMENT TABLE			
9			(Interest from 10.0% - 17.0%)			
10			(Principal from $8,000 - $12,000)			
11						
12		$8,000.00	$9,000.00	$10,000.00	$11,000.00	$12,000.00
13	10.0%					
14	11.0%					
15	12.0%					
16	13.0%					
17	14.0%					
18	15.0%					
19	16.0%					
20	17.0%					

Where:

Column A   Contains the values which represent the interest rates.

Row 12   Contains the values which represent the principal.

The layout of the table is almost complete. Only the function to be calculated requires entry. The function itself or a reference (by cell or range name) to it must be entered in the upper left corner of the table—in this example, cell A12.

Task	Procedure	
	Cell Location	Enter
Enter the cell reference.	A12	+B7 [R]
Select Data Table 2.		/DT2A12..F20[R]
Enter INTEREST as Input cell 1.		[F3] INTEREST[R]
Enter PRINCIPAL as Input cell 2.		[F3] PRINCIPAL[R]

Your screen should look like the example below.

Save as TABLE2.

	A	B	C	D	E	F
1	Loan Data					
2						
3	Principal	$10,000.00				
4	Interest	5.0%				
5	Term	5				
6						
7	Payment	$2,309.75				
8			PAYMENT TABLE			
9			(Interest from 10.0% - 17.0%)			
10			(Principal from $8,000 - $12,000)			
11						
12	+B7	$8,000.00	$9,000.00	$10,000.00	$11,000.00	$12,000.00
13		10.0%	2,110.38	2,374.18	2,637.97	2,901.77	3,165.57
14		11.0%	2,164.56	2,435.13	2,705.70	2,976.27	3,246.84
15		12.0%	2,219.28	2,496.69	2,774.10	3,051.51	3,328.92
16		13.0%	2,274.52	2,558.83	2,843.15	3,127.46	3,411.77
17		14.0%	2,330.27	2,621.55	2,912.84	3,204.12	3,495.40
18		15.0%	2,386.52	2,684.84	2,983.16	3,281.47	3,579.79
19		16.0%	2,443.28	2,748.68	3,054.09	3,359.50	3,664.91
20		17.0%	2,500.51	2,813.07	3,125.64	3,438.20	3,750.77

On Your Own: The Payment Function

Change the table you just created to show payments on principal of $10,000 from 5% through 12%.

Case Study #5: Financial Functions

You are in the market for a used boat, and cannot decide between a Mariner at $24,500 and a Tartan at $39,900. The owner of the Tartan is asking for $2,000 down and will finance the balance at 6% per year over five years. The Mariner is being sold by a dealer, who offers financing at 9.99% over 20 years, with no down payment. Which do you think is the better deal?

APPENDIX

The Lotus 1-2-3 Screen

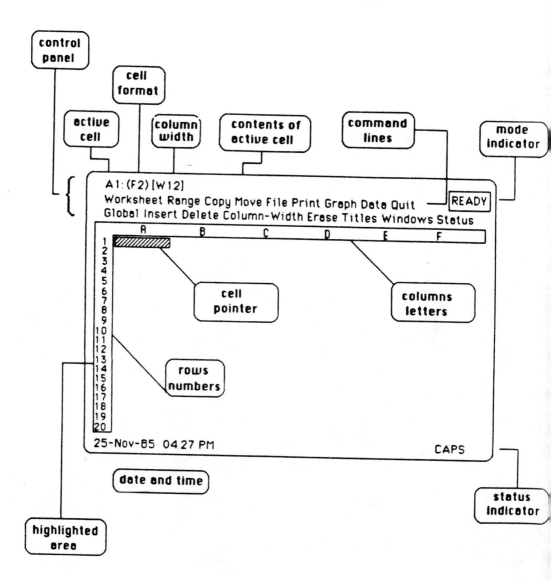

Worksheet Commands

Global   makes changes, usually formatting, to entire
          worksheet

Insert   inserts rows and columns

Delete   deletes rows and columns

Column   alters column-width for entire worksheet

Erase   erase worksheet from memory

Titles   fixes (freezes) titles horizontally, vertically
          or both

Window   opens a second worksheet window

Status   gives information about worksheet size
          and remaining memory

Page   inserts a page break in the current cell

Cell Ranges and Range Commands

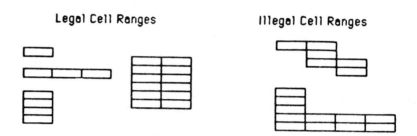

Range Commands

Format	format numbers, dates, text
Label	format labels (right, left, center)
Erase	erase cell or cell range
Name	name a cell or cell range
Justify	format a long text entry
Protect	protect a cell or cell range
Unprotect	unprotect a cell or cell range
Input	limits cell entry to unprotect cells
Value	copies values without copying formulas
Transpose	converts rows to columns and vice versa

Lotus Mathematical Functions

@SUM   Computes the numbers in a cell range.

@COUNT   Returns the number of entries in a range.

@MIN   Returns the minimum value in a range.

@MAX   Returns the maximum value in a range.

@AVG   Computes the average of a cell range.

@SQRT   Computes the square root of a cell entry.

@ROUND   Rounds a cell entry to a specified number of digits.

@INT   Returns the integer portion of an entry.

@ABS   Returns the absolute value of an entry.

@RND   Generates a random number.

@MOD   Returns the remainder from division.

@PI   Returns the value of pi to 15 decimal places.

Twelve Important Lotus Commands

Task	Procedure	
Retrieve a file from disk	/FR	File Retrieve
Save a file to disk	/FS	File Save
Erase a worksheet	/WEY	Worksheet Erase Yes
Insert/Delete rows/columns	/WI	Worksheet Insert
	/WD	Worksheet Delete
Alter all column widths	/WGC	Worksheet Global Column
Alter one column width	/WCS	Worksheet Column
Format all numerical entries	/WGF	Worksheet Global Format
Format a range of numbers	/RF	Range Format
Format all label entries	/WGL	Worksheet Global Label
Format a range of labels	/RL	Range Label
Name a range of cells	/RNC	Range Name Create
Format a date	/RFD	Range Format Date

ANSWERS TO QUICK CHECK EXERCISES

UNIT I: INTRODUCTION TO ELECTRONIC SPREADSHEETS

1. Press [Home].

2. D7.

3. 16 cells.

4. /FILE RETRIEVE and type the name of the file; then press [R].

5. /FILE SAVE and type the name of the file; then press [R].

UNIT II: BUILDING A SPREADSHEET

Part 1: Building a Spreadsheet

1. Values (numbers, formulas, functions) and labels (text).

2. '—left justify.
   ^—center.
   "—right justify.
   \—repeating.

3. Retype it; use [F2] to edit the cell.

4. With cell pointer in F5, enter +D5-E5[R].

5. With cell pointer in A12, enter @SUM(A6..A10)[R].

Part 2: Getting Help

1. The panel at the top of the screen, which contains the current cell address, cell contents, and command menu.

2. The cell under the cell pointer, its address appears in the first line of the control panel.

3. Ready—enter a value, label or formula.
   Edit—edit the current cell.
   See the list of mode indicators for others (page 25).

4. [Esc].

5. [F1].

6. [/].

UNIT III: FORECASTING WITH LOTUS

1. F2.

2. What if the inflation rate was not the same in each quarter?

3. Income as an input cell would allow profits and percent of expenses to be computed.

4. a. /WORKSHEET INSERT ROW A20 [R]
   b. +B20*(1+$F$2).
   c. Absolutely.
   d. Relatively.

5. /FILE LIST.

UNIT IV: FORMATTING SPREADSHEETS

1. TEXT.

2. Asterisks will be displayed.

3. /WORKSHEET GLOBAL FORMAT.

4. /RANGE LABEL CENTER A3..F3 [R].

5. Left-justified.

6. /WORKSHEET GLOBAL COLUMN-WIDTH 12 [R].

7. /WORKSHEET WINDOW VERTICAL.

8. Makes both windows scroll together.

UNIT V: DISPLAYING SPREADSHEET DATA

1. /PRINT PRINTER RANGE (specify range) ALIGN GO.

2. Line, bar, XY, stacked bar, and pie.

3. /GRAPH NAME CREATE allows a particular graph to be named and stores the settings as part of the spreadsheet when the file is saved; several types of graphs using the same data can be used without resetting all the graph options. /GRAPH SAVE creates a separate .PIC file, which is necessary in order to print the graph.

UNIT VII: DATABASE MANAGEMENT

1. Records.

2. /DATA FILL B1..B21[R] 2[R] 40[R].

3. Lastname as primary key, Firstname as secondary key; State as primary key, Zipcode as secondary key; Zipcode as primary key.

4. Set up criterion range; set up output range.

5. Immediately under salary in the criterion range, enter +F11>20000.

6. Save time and space in referring to ranges; help document the formulas (make them easier to read).

ANSWERS TO ON YOUR OWN EXERCISES

UNIT I: Loading and Exiting Lotus 1-2-3

After you have made the changes, your spreadsheet should look like this:

1	Name:	Margaret Brown	
2	Date:	<Today's Date>	
3	Subject:	Employee Ages and Salaries	
4			
5	Name	Age	Salary
6			
7	Adams, John	12	35000
8	Smith, Susan	13	42000
9	Jones, Randy	9	24500

UNIT II: Using Prefixes

1. Since the first entry was a number, Lotus treated the cell contents as a value. The slashes and dashes were treated as operators, and the result of the calculation was displayed in the cell.

    To correct, simply put a label prefix in front of the first number, for example '12/12/89 or ^12-12-89 or "12/12/89, depending on where you want the entry justified in the cell.

2. It could not be entered into the cell because the cell contents were mixed (both values and labels). Lotus went into Edit mode to allow you to make the cell contents either all values or all labels. In this case 1990 is treated as a label (we do not wish to calculate it), so edit the entry by placing a label prefix in front of it, for example '1990 Budget.

3. B3+B4+B5 appears in the cell. Since the first entry was the letter B, Lotus read the contents as a label rather than as a formula, and simply furnished what you typed, rather than returning the value of the formula. Fix it by placing a value prefix, preferably the plus sign, before the B, for example +B3.

UNIT III: Asking What-If Questions

Although your spreadsheet will not look exactly like the one below, the principle is the same. The sample shows the formulas and functions used.

	A	B	C	D	E
1	Date:		January 1, 1988		0.07
2	Name:		Samantha Pirelli		0.1
3	Subject:		Personal Budget		
4					
5					
6			Current Year	Next Year	
7					
8	INCOME		25000		+C8*(1+$E$1)
9					
10	EXPENSES				
11	Auto		4589		+C11*(1+$E$2)
12	Mortgage		8400		+C12*(1+$E$2)
13	Insurance		700		+C13*(1+$E$2)
14	Food		3765		+C14*(1+$E$2)
15	Clothing		7430		+C15*(1+$E$2)
16					
17	TOTAL EXPENSES	@SUM(C11..C15)			@SUM(E11..E15)
18					
19	NET INCOME		+C8-C17		+E8-E17

UNIT IV: Using Formats and Formulas

	A	B	C	D	E	F	G
1	Date:	January 1, 1988			0.07		
2	Name:	Samantha Pirelli			0.1		
3	Subject:	Personal Budget			% save		0.07
4							
5		Current Year			Next Year	Difference	New Budget
6							
7		25,000.00			26,750.00	+E7-C7	
8							
9							
10	Auto	4,589.00			5,047.90	+E10-C10	+E10-(E10*$G$3)
11	Mortgage	8,400.00			9,240.00	+E11-C11	+E11-(E11*$G$3)
12	Insurance	700.00			770.00	+E12-C12	+E12-(E12*$G$3)
13	Food	3,765.00			4,141.50	+E13-C13	+E13-(E13*$G$3)
14	Clothing	7,430.00			8,173.00	+E14-C14	+E14-(E14*$G$3)
15							
16	TOTAL	24,884.00			27,372.40	+E16-C16	@SUM(G10..G14)
17							
18	NET INCOME	116.00			(622.40)		
19							
20	% SAVING ON EXPENSES NEEDED				+F7/F16		

UNIT V: Graphics Enhancements

1. Select PrintGraph from access menu or type PGRAPH at DOS prompt.

2. Select Image EXPPIE [R] SETTINGS IMAGE FONT 1 SCRIPT [Spacebar] to mark, then [R] to select. Repeat sequence for Font 2.

3. Select SIZE FULL QUIT QUIT SAVE ALIGN GO.

UNIT VI: Summary Worksheet

1. Retrieve DEPT1.

2. Enter new salary values.

3. Save file as DEPT1B.

4. Retrieve SUMMARY1.

5. With cursor on B11, /FILE COMBINE COPY NAMED-
   SPECIFIED-RANGE, Data, DEPT1B [R], /FS SUM1.

UNIT VII: Data Query and Extraction

	A	B	C	D	E	F	G
1	Training in New York						
2							
3							
4	1 White	Mark		14-Sep-65	Manager	42000.00	22.9
5	2 Warner	Robert		30-Jun-68	Manager	38750.00	20.1
6	3 Wagner	Thomas		05-Aug-69	Manager	38000.00	19.0
7	4 Gordon	Jose		22-May-78	Supervisor	25500.00	10.2
8							
9	Training at Home Office						
10							
11	5 Dean	Fred		16-Jul-78	Manager	34000.00	10.0
12	6 Bonfield	Arturo		25-Dec-78	Supervisor	26500.00	9.6
13	7 Fried	Sally		11-Dec-82	Supervisor	23000.00	5.6
14	8 O'Brien	Sarah		22-Nov-83	Supervisor	22500.00	4.7
15							

UNIT VIII: Macro Wish List

What did you list?

UNIT IX: Writing and Executing Macros

This macro enters the setup string \015 to print 15 pitch after
setting the right margin to 132.

/PPR{?}.{?}~OMR132~S\015~QAGQ

UNIT X: Autoload Macro

Refer to Automatic Loading of Worksheets:

1. Make a copy of MACTEMP, naming it AUTO123.

2. Test it by quitting 123 and reloading it.

3. Design the documentation section, entering the data you need, reformatting cells, resetting column widths, and editing macros as needed.

4. Save it as Auto123.

UNIT XI: Auto-executing Macro Menu

1. Load Auto123.

2. Go to Macros.

3. Below the label \M enter \0 (don't forget the label prefix).

4. Name the same range for \0 as used for \M, {MENUBRANCH MENU}.

5. Save the file.

6. Quit and start 1-2-3 again.

UNIT XII: RANGE PROTECT

1. /RANGE PROTECT B19..E20.

2. /RANGE ERASE B19..E20 does erase that range, so the RANGE PROTECT apparently did not work.

3. Issue the command again, and before typing in the range, press [F1] to get the context-sensitive help screen. Note that to protect a cell from being changed or erased, not only must it be protected, but protection must be turned on with the WORKSHEET GLOBAL PROTECTION ENABLE command.

4. Restore the data by doing a RANGE TRANSPOSE DATA, then issue /WGPE and try to erase the range again.

5. UNPROTECT the RANGE.

UNIT XIII: Functions

15	CODE	HIREDATE	CODE3 HIRED SINCE 1985	
16	+F6=3	+J6>=@DATE(85,1,1)	Number Hired	3
17			% of Total Code 3	50%

15 CODE3 HIRED SINCE 1985
16 Number Hired   @DCOUNT($DATABASE,5,S15..T16)
17 % of Total Code 3 +X16/@DCOUNT($DATABASE,5,S15..S16)

UNIT XIV: Financial Functions

1. At A12, issue /DATA TABLE RESET.

2. At A13, do DATA FILL starting at 5%, steps of 1% to A20.

3. At A12, issue /DATA TABLE 2 for A12..F20, using [F3] to display ranges, choosing INTEREST and PRINCIPAL.

	A	B	C	D	E	F
6						
7	Payment	$2,309.75				
8				PAYMENT TABLE		
9			(Interest from 10.0% - 17.0%)			
10			(Principal from $8,000 - $12,000)			
11						
12	+B7		$8,000.00	$9,000.00	$10,000.00	$11,000.00	$12,000.00
13		5.0%	1,847.80	2,078.77	2,309.75	2,540.72	2,771.70
14		6.0%	1,899.17	2,136.57	2,373.96	2,611.36	2,848.76
15		7.0%	1,951.13	2,195.02	2,438.91	2,682.80	2,926.69
16		8.0%	2,003.65	2,254.11	2,504.56	2,755.02	3,005.48
17		9.0%	2,056.74	2,313.83	2,570.92	2,828.02	3,085.11
18		10.0%	2,110.38	2,374.18	2,637.97	2,901.77	3,165.57
19		11.0%	2,164.56	2,435.13	2,705.70	2,976.27	3,246.84
20		12.0%	2,219.28	2,496.69	2,774.10	3,051.51	3,328.92

ANSWERS TO CASE STUDIES

Case Study #1: Personal Budget

	A	B	C	D
1	Date:		January 1, 1988	
2	Name:		Samantha Pirelli	
3	Subject:		Personal Budget	
4				
5				
6				
7				
8	INCOME		25000	
9				
10	EXPENSES			
11	Auto		4589	
12	Mortgage		8400	
13	Insurance		700	
14	Food		3765	
15	Clothing		7430	
16				
17	TOTAL EXPENSES		@SUM(C11..C15)	
18				
19	NET INCOME		+C8-C17	

Case Study #2: Lease versus Buy Option

Both the numbers and the formulas are shown for four portions of the spreadsheet.

SCREEN 1 — NUMBERS

	A	B	C	D	E
1	Answer to Case Study #2			LEASE VS. BUY OPTION	
2					
3					
4				BUY	
5			--		
6	Items	# To Purchase	Unit Cost	Total Cost	Yr.Service
7					
8	CPU	5	2,250.00	11,250.00	1687.5
9	Monitor/mono	2	110.00	220.00	33
10	Monitor/color	3	425.00	1,275.00	191.25
11	Hard disk	1	1,100.00	1,100.00	165
12	Printer/laser	1	950.00	950.00	142.5
13	Printer/dot	4	400.00	1,600.00	240
14	Software	5	1,900.00	9,500.00	1425
15					
16	TOTAL			25895	3884.25
17					
18	TOTAL COST TO BUY (cost + 5 yr service)				45316.25
19					============

SCREEN 1 — FORMULAS

	A	B	C	D	E	A
1	Answer to Case Study #2			LEASE VS. BUY OPTION	1	Answer
2					2	
3						
4				BUY		
5			--			
6	Items	# To Purchase	Unit Cost	Total Cost	Yr.Service	
7						
8	CPU	5	2250	+B8*C8	+$D$8*0.15	
9	Monitor/mono	2	110	+B9*C9	+$D$9*0.15	
10	Monitor/color	3	425	+B10*C10	+$D$10*0.15	
11	Hard disk	1	1100	+B11*C11	+$D$11*0.15	
12	Printer/laser	1	950	+B12*C12	+$D$12*0.15	
13	Printer/dot	4	400	+B13*C13	+$D$13*0.15	
14	Software	5	1900	+B14*C14	+$D$14*0.15	
15						
16	TOTAL			@SUM(D8..D14)	@SUM(E8..E14)	
17						
18	TOTAL COST TO BUY (cost + 5 yr service)				+D16+(5*E16)	
19					================	

SCREEN 2 — NUMBERS

	A	B	C	D	E
20					
21	Items			LEASE	
22			--		
23				5 yr lease	10% purchase
24					
25	CPU			19687.5	1125
26	Monitor/mono			385	22
27	Monitor/color			2231.25	127.5
28	Hard disk			1925	110
29	Printer/laser			1662.5	95
30	Printer/dot			2800	160
31	Software			16625	950
32					
33	TOTAL			45316.25	2589.5
34					
35	TOTAL COST TO LEASE				47905.75
36					============
37	LEASE VS BUY (Lease less buy)				2589.5

SCREEN 2 — FORMULAS

	A	B	C	D	E
20					
21	Items			LEASE	
22				--	
23				5 yr lease	10% purchase
24					
25	CPU			+D8*0.35*5	+D8*0.1
26	Monitor/mono			+D9*0.35*5	+D9*0.1
27	Monitor/color			+D10*0.35*5	+D10*0.1
28	Hard disk			+D11*0.35*5	+D11*0.1
29	Printer/laser			+D12*0.35*5	+D12*0.1
30	Printer/dot			+D13*0.35*5	+D13*0.1
31	Software			+D14*0.35*5	+D14*0.1
32					
33	TOTAL			@SUM(D25..D31)	@SUM(E31..E25)
34					
35	TOTAL COST TO LEASE				+D33+E33
36					================
37	LEASE VS BUY (Lease less buy)				+E35-E18

SCREEN 3 — NUMBERS

	G	H	I	J	K	L
1						
2						
3						
4			ANNUAL CASH FLOW--BUY OPTION			
5	--					
6	Year 1	Year 2	Year 3	Year 4	Year 5	Total
7						
8	12,937.50	1,687.50	1,687.50	1,687.50	1,687.50	19,687.50
9	253.00	33.00	33.00	33.00	33.00	385.00
10	1,466.25	191.25	191.25	191.25	191.25	2,231.25
11	1,265.00	165.00	165.00	165.00	165.00	1,925.00
12	1,092.50	142.50	142.50	142.50	142.50	1,662.50
13	1,840.00	240.00	240.00	240.00	240.00	2,800.00
14	10,925.00	1,425.00	1,425.00	1,425.00	1,425.00	16,625.00
15						
16	$29,779.25	$3,884.25	$3,884.25	$3,884.25	$3,884.25	$45,316.25

SCREEN 3 — FORMULAS

ANNUAL CASH FLOW--BUY OPTION

Year 1	Year 2	Year 3	Year 4	Year 5	Total
+D8+E8	+$D$8*0.15	+$D$8*0.15	+$D$8*0.15	+$D$8*0.15	@SUM(G8..K8)
+D9+E9	+$D$9*0.15	+$D$9*0.15	+$D$9*0.15	+$D$9*0.15	@SUM(G9..K9)
+D10+E10	+$D$10*0.15	+$D$10*0.15	+$D$10*0.15	+$D$10*0.15	@SUM(G10..K10)
+D11+E11	+$D$11*0.15	+$D$11*0.15	+$D$11*0.15	+$D$11*0.15	@SUM(G11..K11)
+D12+E12	+$D$12*0.15	+$D$12*0.15	+$D$12*0.15	+$D$12*0.15	@SUM(G12..K12)
+D13+E13	+$D$13*0.15	+$D$13*0.15	+$D$13*0.15	+$D$13*0.15	@SUM(G13..K13)
+D14+E14	+$D$14*0.15	+$D$14*0.15	+$D$14*0.15	+$D$14*0.15	@SUM(G14..K14)
@SUM(G8..G14)	@SUM(H8..H14)	@SUM(I8..I14)	@SUM(J8..J14)	@SUM(K8..K14)	@SUM(L8..L14)

SCREEN 4 — NUMBERS

	G	H	I	J	K	L
20						
21			ANNUAL CASH FLOW--LEASE OPTION			
22	---					
23	Year 1	Year 2	Year 3	Year 4	Year 5	Total
24						
25	3,937.50	3,937.50	3,937.50	3,937.50	5,062.50	20,812.50
26	77.00	77.00	77.00	77.00	99.00	407.00
27	446.25	446.25	446.25	446.25	573.75	2,358.75
28	385.00	385.00	385.00	385.00	495.00	2,035.00
29	332.50	332.50	332.50	332.50	427.50	1,757.50
30	560.00	560.00	560.00	560.00	720.00	2,960.00
31	3,325.00	3,325.00	3,325.00	3,325.00	4,275.00	17,575.00
32						
33	$9,063.25	$9,063.25	$9,063.25	$9,063.25	$11,652.75	$47,905.75

SCREEN 4 — FORMULAS

ANNUAL CASH FLOW--LEASE OPTION

Year 1	Year 2	Year 3	Year 4	Year 5	Total
+$D$8*0.35	+$D$8*0.35	+$D$8*0.35	+$D$8*0.35	+E25+J25	@SUM(G25..K25)
+$D$9*0.35	+$D$9*0.35	+$D$9*0.35	+$D$9*0.35	+E26+J26	@SUM(G26..K26)
+$D$10*0.35	+$D$10*0.35	+$D$10*0.35	+$D$10*0.35	+E27+J27	@SUM(G27..K27)
+$D$11*0.35	+$D$11*0.35	+$D$11*0.35	+$D$11*0.35	+E28+J28	@SUM(G28..K28)
+$D$12*0.35	+$D$12*0.35	+$D$12*0.35	+$D$12*0.35	+E29+J29	@SUM(G29..K29)
+$D$13*0.35	+$D$13*0.35	+$D$13*0.35	+$D$13*0.35	+E30+J30	@SUM(G30..K30)
+$D$14*0.35	+$D$14*0.35	+$D$14*0.35	+$D$14*0.35	+E31+J31	@SUM(G31..K31)

@SUM(G25..G31) @SUM(H25..H31) @SUM(I25..I31) @SUM(J25..J31)@SUM(K25..K31) @SUM(L25..L31)

Case Study #3: Databases

	A	B	C	D	E	F	G
2			The Box Factory				
3							
4		YTD Sales:	$72,339.63				
5							
6							
7	ID	Client Name	Address	City	ST	Zip	Total
8							
9	A	Hero Dairy	135 Milky Way	Dairyland	WI	109660	2,459.45
10	A	Helen's Gifts	12 Main St.	Scenic	SD	115560	827.90
11	A	Pet Rocks	557 Nugget Ct.	Rock City	IL	122140	1,165.23
12	A	Al's Auto Parts	214 Speed Drive	Glen Cove	NY	23084	1,047.25
13	A	Speedo Printing	669 Grove Ave.	Victor	ID	166910	6,556.97
14	B	Surf Suits	982 Ocean Ave.	Cocoa Beach	FL	65862	9,764.89
15	B	United Citrus	227 Thomas St.	Tangerine	FL	65554	13,689.55
16	B	Aloe Products	784 Sunset Way	Key West	FL	66080	1,189.50
17	B	Grant Seafood	116 Dixie Hwy.	Grant	FL	65898	217.56
18	B	Terry's Groves	12 Main St.	Frostproof	FL	67686	13,850.00
19	C	National Emblem	658 Flag Drive	Old Glory	TX	159080	556.97
20	C	Western Souvenir	655 Everett St.	Broken Bow	OK	149456	3,178.96
21	C	Tia Maria Foods	946 Buena Vista	Tortilla Flat	AZ	170580	6,211.99

Case Study #4: The Lookup Function

6	SALE	DISCOUNT	NET		CASH DISCOUNT TABLE	
7						
8	$5,656.52	$169.70	$5,486.82		100	0.1
9	$7,450.29	$223.51	$7,226.78		500	0.05
10	$186.00	$18.60	$167.40		5000	0.03
11	$52,778.97	$0.00	$52,778.97		10000	

6	SALE	DISCOUNT	NET
7			
8	$5,656.52	(@VLOOKUP(A8,$F$8..$G$11,1))*A8	+A8-B8
9	$7,450.29	(@VLOOKUP(A9,$F$8..$G$11,1))*A9	+A9-B9
10	$186.00	(@VLOOKUP(A10,$F$8..$G$11,1))*A10	+A10-B10
11	$52,778.97	(@VLOOKUP(A11,$F$8..$G$11,1))*A11	+A11-B11

Case Study #5: Financial Functions

	A	B	C
1		MARINER	TARTAN
2		-------------	-------------
3	Principal	$22,500.00	$39,900.00
4	Interest	6.0%	9.99%
5	Term	5.0	20.0
6			
7	Payment	$5,341.42	$4,683.44
8			
9	TOTAL COST	$28,707.10	$93,668.81

		B	C
7	Payment	@PMT(B3,B4,B5)	@PMT(C3,C4,C5)
8			
9	TOTAL COST	(B7*5)+2000	+C7*20

Index